Teacher-Centered

Professional Development

Gabriel Díaz-Maggioli

Association for Supervision and Curriculum Development
Alexandria, Virginia USA

Association for Supervision and Curriculum Development
1703 N. Beauregard St. • Alexandria, VA 22311-1714 USA
Telephone: 800-933-2723 or 703-578-9600 • Fax: 703-575-5400
Web site: http://www.ascd.org • E-mail: member@ascd.org

Gene R. Carter, *Executive Director;* Nancy Modrak, *Director of Publishing;* Julie Houtz, *Director of Book Editing & Production;* Ernesto Yermoli, *Project Manager;* Reece Quiñones, *Senior Graphic Designer;* Keith Demmons, *Desktop Publishing Specialist;* Vivian Coss, *Production Specialist*

s5/04

Paperback ISBN: 0-87120-859-8 • ASCD product #104021
e-books: netLibrary ISBN 1-4166-0015-9 • ebrary ISBN 1-4166-0016-7 • Retail PDF ISBN 1-4166-0279-8
....
Library of Congress Cataloging-in-Publication Data

Díaz-Maggioli, Gabriel, 1963-
  Teacher-centered professional development / Gabriel Díaz-Maggioli.
     p. cm.
  Includes bibliographical references and index.
  ISBN 0-87120-859-8 (pbk. : alk. paper)
  1. Teachers—In-service training—United States. I. Title.

  LB1731.D53 2004
  370'.71'55—dc22
                                2004004637

10 09 08 07 06   12 11 10 9 8 7 6 5 4 3 2

Teacher-Centered Professional Development

To Teresa, who started me on the path to personal and professional growth, and in loving memory of Michael

To the 2002–2003 Humphrey Fellows at Penn State University

Acknowledgments

The author would like to thank the following colleagues for their contributions to this book:

Dr. James Nolan of Penn State University for his inspiration, generosity, and encouragement;

Dr. Debra Freedman of Penn State University for her suggestions, inspiration, and professionalism;

Marianne Posner for her insightful comments on the manuscript and her friendship and camaraderie;

Mzia Mikeladze for her interest in collaborative professional development and for listening and responding to my ideas;

Scott Willis and the editorial staff at ASCD, especially Ernesto Yermoli, for providing great resources and support;

And finally, to all the teachers and student teachers in Uruguay and the United States who provided ideas, insights, and examples for the manuscript. Their stories are woven into this book and have convinced me that a better future for all our students is possible.

– 1 –

Professional Development Today

"Let's face it: Professional development, as we have known it for years now, has yielded little or no positive effects on student learning." Thus complain the many weary professionals who flinch at the mere mention of the word "workshop." In the collective imagination, the term "professional development day" conjures only images of coffee breaks, consultants in elegant outfits, and schools barren of kids.

Of course, professional development was never intended to trigger such pessimistic reactions. Even critics of the professional development movement admit that all forms of teacher development, whether effective or not, have at their core the noble intention of improving student learning. We might disagree with the implementation processes available, but not with their purpose. Indeed, when correctly implemented, they actually yield the results intended. In this era of high-stakes testing and increased accountability, it is necessary to reposition professional development so that the collective efforts of teachers, students, and administrators result in enhanced learning for all members of the teaching community.

1

Current professional development practices are generally constricted by the following stumbling blocks:

1. **Top-down decision making.** Traditionally, professional development arrangements are made by administrators and consultants rather than teachers. By muffling the teachers' voices and placing priority on administrative needs, these programs become a burden to professionals instead of a welcome solution to classroom problems.

2. **The idea that teachers need to be "fixed."** Too often, professional development is guided by the erroneous idea that if students don't learn, it's because their teachers don't know how to teach. Myriad approaches to teaching have surfaced over the past fifteen years or so, all claiming to be the ultimate solution for teaching problems. However, when we listen in awe at the stories of classroom teachers—stories of passion and commitment, strife and success, dedication and love—it's easy to wonder what kind of fixing these teachers might need.

3. **Lack of ownership of the professional development process and its results.** Given that their voices are not generally heeded during professional development, teachers rightly question their investment in programs that were built behind their backs yet are aimed at changing the way they do things.

4. **The technocratic nature of professional development content.** More often than not, teachers in professional development programs are taught techniques that they are expected to replicate in the classroom. Most of these methods, however effective, are standardized for communication purposes and serve the needs of

teachers and learners in specific contexts. In attempting to transfer these practices into their classrooms, teachers need to invest considerably more effort than the professional development planners originally anticipated.

5. **Universal application of classroom practices regardless of subject, student age, or level of cognitive development.** It is not uncommon to hear of school districts that run the same professional development programs for all grade levels. While certain teaching practices and learning principles might be suitable across the board, a one-size-fits-all approach, though economical, has been proven totally ineffective.

6. **Lack of variety in the delivery modes of professional development.** Once a decision is made to invest in professional development, the cheapest format is often chosen for the purpose—usually a lecture, workshop, or seminar. It is ironic that so much has been written about the importance of differentiated instruction in the classroom; when it comes to instruction for teachers, undifferentiated approaches usually prevail.

7. **Inaccessibility of professional development opportunities.** Professional development opportunities seldom reach teachers when they are really needed. When teachers do not help plan and deliver professional development programs, their needs can go unmet. This may help explain why only a small percentage of teachers seems able to transfer the content covered in a workshop to the classrooms.

8. **Little or no support in transferring professional development ideas to the classroom.** Transferring new ideas to the classroom

is perhaps one of the most difficult tasks a teacher faces. A lot of effort is put into helping preservice teachers bridge the gap between theory and practice; we may wonder why the same support systems are not available to in-service teachers as well.

9. **Standardized approaches to professional development that disregard the varied needs and experiences of teachers.** Researchers have pointed out that teachers go through certain developmental stages as they progress in their careers, each of which triggers specific needs and crises that they must address (Fessler & Christensen, 1992; Furlong & Maynard, 1995; Huberman, 1989). The standardized nature of traditional professional development programs assumes that all teachers should perform at the same level, regardless of their particular experience and needs.

10. **Lack of systematic evaluation of professional development.** Given the complex nature of teacher competence, assessing development often seems impossible. As a result, many professional development programs are not evaluated, nor are their results communicated to other communities. Teachers would be right to take offense at this. A learning organization should yield knowledge that enriches not only the immediate community, but the profession as a whole. It is a disservice to the teaching community when we fail to probe the effectiveness of established programs and overlook their results.

11. **Little or no acknowledgment of the learning characteristics of teachers among professional development planners.** Most professional development models for teachers ignore the fact that teachers possess unique learning characteristics that must be

accounted for if the programs are to be successful. Though the characteristics of adult learners have been the focus of research for over a century now (Brookfield, 1986; Vella, 1994), they are too often overlooked.

My vision of professional development is grounded in faith in teachers, the institutions they work for, and the power of the broader community of educators around the country and the globe. Effective professional development should be understood as a job-embedded commitment that teachers make in order to further the purposes of the profession while addressing their own particular needs. It should follow the principles that guide the learning practices of experienced adults, in teaching communities that foster cooperation and shared expertise. Teacher success stories are living theories of educational quality and should be shared with the wider educational community for the benefit of all involved.

Figure 1.1 summarizes my vision of professional development in contrast to more traditional practices.

Acknowledging Teaching Styles

Professional development can be defined as a career-long process in which educators fine-tune their teaching to meet student needs. As such, it directly tackles teachers' teaching styles—the patterns of decisions teachers make when mediating their students' learning. Butler (1984) defines learning styles as "a set of attitudes and actions that open a formal and informal world of learning to students. It is a subtle force that influences a student's access to learning and teaching by establishing perimeters around acceptable learning procedures, processes, and products" (pp. 51–52). But just as learners learn

1.1 Traditional vs. Visionary Professional Development

Characteristics of Traditional Professional Development	Characteristics of Visionary Professional Development
• Top-down decision-making • A "fix-it" approach • Lack of program ownership among teachers • Prescriptive ideas • One-size-fits-all techniques • Fixed and untimely delivery methods • Little or no follow–up • Decontextualized programs • Lack of proper evaluation • Pedagogical (child-centered) instruction	• Collaborative decision-making • A growth-driven approach • Collective construction of programs • Inquiry-based ideas • Tailor-made techniques • Varied and timely delivery methods • Adequate support systems • Context-specific programs • Proactive assessment • Andragogical (adult-centered) instruction

according to a particular style, so do teachers exhibit particular teaching styles. Most researchers agree that teaching styles operate along a continuum that ranges from teacher-centered to student-centered. In characterizing these styles, researchers tend to focus on such criteria as control over time and procedures, student involvement, and materials used in class.

The issue of teaching styles is far more complex than it appears at first. First of all, it is necessary to acknowledge that the term itself refers to the way teachers perform in the classroom—that is, to teacher behavior. These behaviors are contingent on a multitude of factors that affect how teachers go about their daily chores. As Figure 1.2 shows, teaching styles are the result of interacting personal, professional, knowledge, career, institutional, and curriculum factors.

Overcoming the Crises of Practice

According to Huberman (1989), teachers progress through the following five phases in their careers, each of which includes a crisis they must overcome:

1.2 Factors Affecting Teaching Styles

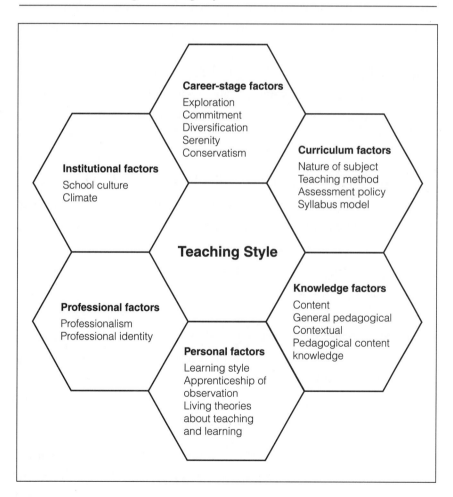

Phase 1: Exploration and stabilization. Teachers develop strategies to cope with day-to-day tasks. There is little or no focus on student learning during this phase, as the teachers are primarily concerned with following rules and plans. *Crisis:* Learning to perceive the messages that the teaching and learning environments send.

Phase 2: Commitment. Teachers take bold steps towards focusing on student learning, developing a repertoire of coping techniques and trying out new ideas. *Crisis:* Learning how best to cater to all students.

Phase 3: Diversification. Teachers begin to question their effectiveness when some of their students fail to learn. Most teachers leave the profession at this stage. *Crisis:* Many need to solve a professional identity crisis.

Phase 4: Serenity or distancing. Teachers resolve the identity crisis in Phase 3 by either confirming their commitment to classroom teaching or by moving into administration or teacher education or by leaving the profession altogether. *Crisis:* If teachers are able to realize their aspirations, they tend to enter a phase of serenity; otherwise, they remain stable but stagnant.

Phase 5: Conservatism and regret. Teachers retire. *Crisis:* For some, regret over the past; for others, refusal to accept that there are other ways to teach besides one's own.

Curriculum Factors

Another factor affecting teaching styles is the school curriculum, which can be defined as the totality of experiences that result in student learning. There are different kinds of curriculum, some intended and some, such as the "hidden curriculum," unintended. Curriculum is built upon the following foundations:

- **Psychological.** How students learn.
- **Epistemological.** The nature and purpose of knowledge.
- **Sociological.** The role of schooling in relation to students, their families, and communities.
- **Didactic.** Practices most likely to result in desired learning outcomes.

All teachers are by definition curriculum developers in that they select, sequence, organize, plan, deliver, and evaluate their students' learning experiences. This process can either inhibit the full expression of teacher learning styles or make them more autonomous. For example, a curriculum focused strongly on high-stakes testing may prompt a teacher to teach to the test at the expense of other important "formational tasks" (Freire, 1998), inhibiting the teacher's style by turning her into a mere deliverer of contents. A curriculum that advocates a dialogic perspective, on the other hand, allows both teacher and student to enter a cycle of action and reflection in which both will grow. In this latter context, the teacher's learning style is open to interaction and the exercise of greater freedom.

School Culture and Climate

Sergiovanni and Starratt (2002) define *school climate* as "the enduring characteristics that describe the psychological character of a particular school, distinguish it from other schools, and influence the behavior of teachers and students, and as the psychological 'feel' that teachers and students have for that school" (p. 82). These "enduring characteristics" include goal focus, communication adequacy, optimal power equalization, resource utilization, cohesiveness, morale, innovativeness, autonomy, adaptation, and problem-solving adequacy. How these characteristics operate within a school determines whether its climate is open (supports learning) or closed (hinders learning).

According to Peterson (2002), *school culture* is "the set of norms, values, and beliefs, rituals and ceremonies, symbols, and stories that make up the 'persona' of the school. These unwritten expectations build up over time as teachers, administrators, parents, and students work together, solve problems, deal with challenges and, at times, cope with failures." School culture is responsible for the way members of a school regard themselves, their relationships with one another, and the institution and its goals.

Hargreaves (1994) proposes the existence of four distinct cultures in educational institutions: isolationist, balkanized, contrived collegial, and collegial. He suggests that educational institutions have a long tradition of isolationism, with teachers operating alone inside their own classrooms. I believe that this isolation accounts for many of the failures we see in schools, and that the ideal school would have a collaborative or collegial culture. According to Petersen (2002), in such a milieu, "teachers, students, and administrators value learning, work to enhance curriculum and instruction, and focus on students. In schools with professional learning communities, the culture possesses:

- A widely shared sense of purpose and values;
- Norms of continuous learning and improvement;
- A commitment to and sense of responsibility for the learning of all students;
- Collaborative, collegial relationships; and
- Opportunities for staff reflection, collective inquiry, and sharing personal practice."

The influence of school cultures on teaching styles cannot be overstated; as with curriculum, they can either hinder or improve teaching.

Professional Factors

Closely linked to the influences of school culture and climate on teaching style is the issue of professionalism. Barker, Kagen, Klemp, Roderick, and Takenaga-Taga (1997) define a true teaching professional as "a teacher who is engaged with a career path that encourages, fosters, and rewards constant professional growth that reflects directly and positively back on classroom practice." This engagement depends upon the teacher's *professional identity:* the way he or she relates to the norms and values of the profession.

Sachs (1999) claims that such a view treats professionalism as "an exclusive rather than an inclusive ideal, and is conservative rather than radical"—thus reducing professional development to the mere acquisition of traits that allow teachers to claim membership in the profession. Because teacher learning stems from reflective involvement with other learners, be they students or fellow teachers, it seems to make more sense for a concept of professionalism to reflect "cooperative action between teachers and other stakeholders" (Sachs, 1999).

Sachs suggests an even more powerful view of teacher professionalism—one that sees it as "negotiated, open, shifting, ambiguous, the result of culturally available meanings and the open-ended power-laden enactment of those meanings in everyday situations"—and identifies "five dimensions of identity:

i. Identity *as negotiated experiences* where we define who we are by the ways we experience our selves through participation as well as the way we and others reify our selves,

ii.   Identity as *community membership* where we define who we are
      by the familiar and the unfamiliar,

iii. Identity *as learning trajectory* where we define who we are by
      where we have been and where are going,

iv.   Identity *as nexus of multi membership* where we define who we
      are by the ways we reconcile our various forms of identity into
      one identity, and

v.   Identity *as a relation between the local and the global* where we
      define who we are by negotiating local ways of belonging to
      broader constellations and manifesting broader styles and
      discourses."

Teaching styles are greatly influenced by the teachers' own ideal-
ization of themselves as teaching professionals. Those who equate
professionalism with adherence to external norms will tend toward
relatively directive and ethnocentric teaching styles; on the other
hand, those who perceive themselves as existing in a dialectical relationship with other professionals, working collectively to build their
professional identities, will necessarily have more constructivist
styles.

Learning Factors

Three learning factors greatly influence teaching styles: the teachers' learning styles, their experience as learners, and the theories
about teaching and learning to which they adhere (Díaz-Maggioli,
1996).

When making decisions, teachers should ideally have the students as their main focus. Too often, however, they teach according
to their own preferred learning methods, rather than according to

what is best for the students. Similarly, teachers tend to emulate the teachers who helped them to learn best when they were in school— though in most cases they don't know *why* the model teachers taught the way they did. Teachers need to be aware of these personal influences and refocus their actions to benefit the students. To do this, they need space to develop their own theories about teaching and learning through professional development with colleagues.

The Teacher's Choice Framework

Planners of professional development programs should bear in mind the following facts:

- Teachers are talented and devoted individuals who have gained enormous experience by interacting with students, and possess a wealth of knowledge that must be explored and shared.
- Teachers differ from one another in terms of their theoretical and professional knowledge and the stages they are at in their careers. This diversity offers a wealth of resources and experience.
- Teachers fulfill different functions in their jobs. They are not only mediators of student learning, but also administrators of student information, counselors on learning, and resources for parents and the broader community. Their professional development should be embedded in their daily schedule; they should not be expected to devote their own free time to programs that are divorced from the context in which they work.

- In order for teachers to develop ownership of professional development, they need to be active participants in its construction, tailoring programs to their needs and motivations.
- Professional development should not be regarded as an administrative duty, but rather as a career-long endeavor aimed at disclosing the factors that contribute to the success of all students and teachers. Mandatory professional development offered only when it is convenient to administrators has little to offer to teachers.
- Professional development will only have an effect on student learning if it involves the entire school community. Knowledge about teaching and learning only makes sense when considered in the context of a teacher's own school culture and climate. The effect of professional development is not measured by the sum of the discrete actions of individual factors and stakeholders, but through an examination of how factors and stakeholders interact with one another.

In order to ensure that professional development is congruent with these facts, educators need an organizational framework based on the unique characteristics and contributions of teachers. The Teacher's Choice Framework (see Figure 1.3) helps teachers make individual and collaborative decisions by having them reflect on practice. For the framework to function effectively, learning communities should promote collaborative reflection on student learning data, which should be gathered and shared across grades and disciplines. Once the data are shared, educators should involve as many stakeholders as possible in planning a professional development program that addresses the needs of all participants.

1.3 The Four Quadrants of the Teacher's Choice Framework

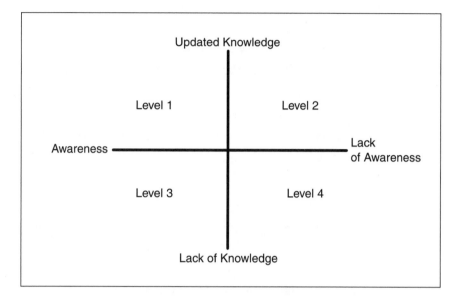

Types and Levels of Awareness

As soon as everyone's needs are clear, it is time to select activities that are suited to each teacher's needs and level of awareness. There are four distinct types of awareness needs that teachers can address through professional development:

- **Technical awareness.** Reflection on particular classroom procedures or teaching methods.
- **Personal awareness.** Reflection on how classroom activity relates to life outside of work.
- **Problematic awareness.** Reflection on how to solve professional problems.
- **Critical awareness.** Reflection on established thoughts, feelings, or actions that have been called into question.

In addition, most teachers fall into one of the following four awareness-level categories:

Level 1. Teachers are aware that they possess up-to-date knowledge and can help other teachers through initiatives such as mentoring, providing on-site teacher training workshops, and expert coaching with colleagues in other levels. They can also develop field notes—narratives of classroom success stories that they share with other teachers for feedback and development.

Level 2. Teachers possess updated knowledge, but are not aware that they do. Those in this category can be involved in mirroring and collaborative coaching by having colleagues come into their classrooms and observe them in order to pinpoint areas of strength. Field notes can serve as a powerful reflection tool for these teachers as well.

Level 3: Teachers are aware of their development needs in specific knowledge areas. Pertinent techniques for this level include engaging in action research, establishing critical development teams, and maintaining dialogue journals.

Level 4: Teachers are unaware of their need to expand their knowledge in certain areas. Appropriate professional development programs for such teachers could include mandated in-house training workshops, mentoring, and expert coaching.

Types of Knowledge

In its 1985 report to the Ford Foundation, the Academy for Educational Development stated the following:

It is reasonable, if not essential, to expect that anyone who intends to teach be: first, educated broadly and well; second, fundamentally knowledgeable about the fields to be taught; third, familiar with how children or adolescents develop, behave, and learn; and fourth, knowledgeable about and skilled in the profession of education to assure quality standards, ethics, responsible conduct, and responsiveness to the educational needs of the greater society. Prospective teachers should also be made aware that continued professional growth depends upon prolonged interaction with peers and others. (p. 25)

Authors such as Shulman (1987), Grossman (1990), and Putnam and Borko (2000) have elaborated on the idea that there are different kinds of teacher knowledge. In a nutshell, teachers are motivated to enter the profession by one or more of the following:

- **Content knowledge.** An interest in the subject matter.
- **General pedagogical knowledge.** An interest in pedagogy.
- **Contextual knowledge.** An interest in students and their communities.

In the course of their work, teachers develop a specific kind of knowledge that differentiates them from subject specialists, pedagogues, or social workers. Grossman (1990) characterizes this kind of knowledge as understanding the purpose for teaching the subject matter, positioning the discipline within the broader school curriculum, and using instructional strategies appropriate for the specific learners and setting. Grossman calls this kind of knowledge "pedagogical content knowledge." All teachers will have moments in their careers when they must focus on increasing their pedagogical content knowledge.

The Teacher's Choice Framework allows teachers with expertise in a certain domain to provide mediation and scaffolding to colleagues whose weaknesses lie in that same area. Teachers enter a cycle of constant development, since teachers can have different awareness levels for different types of knowledge. A teacher well versed in developing a classroom climate conducive to learning, for example, may pair up with one who has classroom management problems—and who in turn might share his or her differentiated instruction expertise with the other teacher. By capitalizing on the internal strengths of its members, the learning community is enriched.

The Teacher's Choice Framework allows teachers to feel reassured about their dual roles as both experts and novices, and "to move along a continuum ranging from inductee to master teacher where increased responsibilities, qualifications, professional development, and performance-based accountability requirements are commensurate with compensation" (Wenglinsky, 2000).

– 2 –

Establishing a Learning Community

We live from birth to death in a world of persons and things which in large measure is what it is because of what has been done and transmitted from previous human activities.

—John Dewey (1997, p. 39)

Joyce's Story

Joyce's first job after graduating was as a Spanish teacher at an urban middle school. Because it was a tenure-track position, she willingly complied with the tenure specifications of her state. She was supervised by the assistant principal during her first year, and took continuing education courses on her subject, much as she had in college. When preparing to observe Joyce's classes, the assistant principal would leave a note on her locker door specifying the date and time he intended to visit. In two of his three visits, the assistant principal met with Joyce before class to discuss the lesson plan. Following the observation they met again, and the assistant principal pointed out areas for Joyce's improvement. Joyce welcomed the feedback and worked hard at building an individual development plan aimed at overcoming her limitations. At the end of her third year at the school, Joyce qualified for tenure, earning a score of "Outstanding" on all the necessary criteria.

Joyce, Two Years Later

Getting tenure was not difficult for Joyce, but her work life has changed dramatically since then, mainly due to the professional development program in her school. Before getting tenure, Joyce was involved in various professional development strategies, often initiated by her peers. She conducted classroom research on communication strategies, and along with another teacher participated in peer-to-peer observations and developed field notes for an article they jointly published in a local journal. Now, as part of her continuing professional development, Joyce is required to take courses at a local university. Though she enjoys the courses, she is most excited about working together with the teachers and students in her school. She regards these opportunities as the best experiences in her professional life so far.

Like many teachers, Joyce has participated in two distinct forms of professional development. The first was enjoyable and useful in that it provided Joyce with a sense of direction during her first year. Looking back, however, she recalls the observations, in-service workshops, and portfolio requirements with some regret; because participation in these strategies was required for tenure, she found that they constrained her full potential. Though useful, this type of professional development contrasts markedly with Joyce's current approach, which is ongoing, proactive, and rooted in her actual needs and the needs of the community. Only now, she feels, can she exercise her full potential as a professional.

Joyce has discovered the joys and pains both of being supervised and of participating in true professional development. Although the supervisory experience of her first years was differentiated and led to her professional growth, Joyce felt she was not able to fully commit to the cycles of observation and feedback—perhaps because they were mandated and she had no say in what she had to do. By contrast, the activities she participated in over the past two years have been much more meaningful. Joyce chose which activities to engage in, and did so at a time beneficial to her own developmental needs. The principal and assistant principal served as mentors and active collaborators for every activity, at times providing guidance, and at other times simply listening to the teachers' concerns. Even when the principal evaluates Joyce's performance at the end of the year, she doesn't feel the overbearing sense of being monitored that she experienced during her first years at the school.

Is Professional Development the Same as Supervision?

Like other educators who engage regularly in professional growth initiatives, Joyce has been involved in both supervision and professional development—terms that are often used interchangeably (Granade Sullivan, 1997; Nolan & Hoover, 2003). Before describing the conditions necessary for the Teacher's Choice Framework to succeed, we must distinguish between these two concepts.

Griffin (1997) provides a list of characteristics that set professional development apart from supervision:

- Because the work of a school is determined by the school's context, supervisory prescriptions—for example, the stages of clinical supervision—cannot contribute to the ultimate aim of staff development, which is change.
- Because staff development is also context-sensitive, those who work at a school are better equipped than outside supervisors to direct their "wisdom of practice" towards school change.
- Staff development should be
  - o Purposeful and articulated. The sense of purpose stems from the school community itself and "is directly opposed to purposes that are formulated within a deficit model of teaching and schooling."
  - o Participatory and collaborative.
  - o Knowledge-based, meaning both "the wisdom of practice that resides in the school as well as more conventional research and theoretical knowledge."
  - o Ongoing, if it is to respond adequately to shifting contexts. Supervision, by contrast, tends to be fragmented and unconnected. This is most evident when teachers are supervised, in their first years of teaching, by different staff—assistant principal, mentors, district supervisors—depending more on the administrators' schedules than the teachers'.
  - o Developmental, in terms of both the participants and the staff development process itself.
  - o Analytic and reflective: "The specific attention to analysis and reflection calls our attention to the importance of knowing one's path and paying attention as it is followed" (pp. 166–169).

Guskey (2000) suggests that staff development is intentional, ongoing, and systematic. Supervision, by contrast, is a *component* of the process of educational change, grounded in the belief that teachers need to be monitored. However, this does not mean that supervision alone can help teachers develop professionally. Because supervision is often a one-size-fits-all approach, it cannot always take into account the individual needs of teachers. Most supervisory practices include evaluation, whether implicitly or explicitly; and even when supervisors are not the evaluators, supervision is designed to achieve preselected goals. The fact that the process has dual purposes—mentoring and evaluation—creates confusion among both supervisors and teachers. Some efforts are being made to separate evaluation from supervision, including calls to select supervisors to monitor teacher development (such as a peer or curriculum area coordinator) and separate evaluators to judge teacher proficiency (such as a building or district administrator).

The ultimate end of supervision is to promote educational reform. Bereiter (2002) usefully elucidates the difference between educational *reform* and educational *transformation:* "Reforms can be imposed from outside, and sometimes have to be, whereas transformation can only come from within" (p. 420). Unlike supervision, professional development provides a fertile breeding ground for educational transformation. Whereas supervision is generally carried out one-on-one, professional development is collaborative and aimed at ensuring that teachers adequately address the needs of students. The voluntary nature of professional development also sets it apart from supervision, which is usually mandated. In addition, professional development emphasizes teacher growth over evaluation, whereas the opposite seems to be true of present-day supervisory practices.

The Teacher's Choice Framework promotes professional development—it is collaborative in nature and embedded in the daily lives of teachers. West (1996) advocates collaborative, job-embedded learning because "buy-in and ownership by workers in the process is increased by collaboration and inclusion. This becomes especially important when diversity exists within the workplace, including not only cultural, racial and socioeconomic diversity but also diversity of thought" (p. 53).

To better understand the professional development process, we need to explore the basic conditions under which it may yield the best results.

Collaborative Work

Though much of the literature on collaborative work focuses more on students than teachers, many of its principles can be extrapolated to benefit teacher professional development (Cohen, 1994; Jacob, Power, & Wan Inn, 2002; Johnson & Johnson, 1984; Kagan, 1994). Over the past twenty years, cooperative learning has gained momentum at all levels of the educational ladder. According to Federman Stein and Hurd (2000), this is because the demands of current work conditions make it almost impossible for people to successfully complete professional tasks on their own.

Drennon and Foucar-Szocki (1996) further explain that "practitioners working with groups of colleagues have the benefit of immediate feedback on their ideas from peers. Learning is enriched as group members draw on the skills and perspectives each brings. As individuals learn, so does the entire group. . . . Authority shifts from outside experts to practitioners inside the program who come to develop and articulate theories grounded in their real-world experience" (p. 72).

Cooperative work deserves special consideration in schools with traditional cultures. It is too easy for schools to become isolationist, with teachers working in the solitude of their classrooms and failing to interact with their peers in addressing student learning. Tyack and Tobin (1994) use the term "grammar of schooling" to describe the pervasive influences of hard-to-change structures and rules affecting school culture and climate; a culture of isolation is one such influence. The standards movement, with its strong emphasis on standardization, content, and testing, helps perpetuate the grammar of schooling and promotes isolationism. When teachers unreflectively focus on the content to be learned by students, or when they teach to the test, students are likely to perceive a discord between the purposes and the uses of their education. In all likelihood, they will also fail to learn in meaningful ways.

On the other hand, when teachers are provided with the means and the time to reflect collectively on their teaching methods, and when they are able to share their teaching styles with each other, results improve and the act of teaching is transformed. Professional teams are instrumental to help teachers make the necessary transition from a culture of isolation to one of cooperation.

West (1996) sees dialogue as a key requirement for collaborative inquiry, noting that it "allows for transforming the thinking that lies behind the words that are said. . . . The goal of dialogue is to help the group bring assumptions to the surface and clarify theories-in-use, which must happen before a shared set of meanings and a common thinking process can be developed" (p. 56).

Characteristics of Collaborative Teams

Successful teams operate according to principles that give them purpose and direction, many of which have been explained at length by authors such as Cohen (1994); Jacob, Power, and Wan Inn (2002); Johnson and Johnson (1984); and Kagan (1994). The principles can be summarized as follows:

Cooperation is a value. In truly cooperative situations, team members actively seek to contribute to the work of others in the team by offering support, challenges, or assessment. One of the goals of the Teacher's Choice Framework is to encourage educators to share their expertise within their department, school, and district. To do this they must rely on each other for support and encouragement.

Teams are heterogeneous. Heterogeneity allows different team members to exercise different levels of expertise. The Teacher's Choice Framework capitalizes on the natural heterogeneity of school faculty to promote sustained interaction during which experts and novices can develop alongside one another. This teamwork fosters sharing, modeling, and scaffolding among all members of staff, contributing to their professional growth.

Team members are interdependent. To quote Jacob, Power, and Wan Inn (2002), "The principle of positive interdependence is the most important principle in cooperative learning. Positive interdependence represents a feeling among group members that what helps one group member benefits all the members and what hurts one member hurts them all" (pp. 31–32).

Team members are individually accountable. Individual members don't abrogate their responsibilities just because they work in teams.

The notion of individual responsibility gives teams coherence, supports cohesion, and helps keep members productive.

Team members interact simultaneously. Simultaneous interaction is inherent in the Teacher's Choice Framework because of the framework's systemic nature. Schools are highly interrelated, so the development needs of individual teachers should be attended to at the same time rather than sequentially.

All team members should have the chance for equal participation. Learning is enriched when everyone has the same opportunities to participate in team activities. However, as Jacob, Power, and Wan Inn (2002) have noted, "It's not realistic to insist on absolute equal participation. On any particular topic or task, there are many legitimate reasons why one student or another has more or less to contribute" (pp. 67–68). The Teacher's Choice Framework allows for equal participation by positioning practitioners in both novice and expert roles, allowing them to build covenants together.

Team members need to learn the core cooperative skills that will help them succeed. Teachers accustomed to the "grammar of schooling" need particular reassurance and direction when developing cooperative skills. As Cohen (1994) puts it, "It is a great mistake to assume that children (or adults) know how to work with each other in a constructive collegial fashion" (p. 34).

Stages of Collaborative Team Development

A variety of researchers have offered differing views on the stages of team development (Federman, Stein & Hurd, 2000; Hills, 2001; Quick, 1992; Tuckman, 1965; Tuckman & Jensen, 1977; Wheelan, 1999). On closer examination, however, the researchers' stages have much in common (see Figure 2.1).

2.1 Four Conceptions of the Stages of Team Development

	Hills (2001)	Wheelan (1999)	Quick (1992)	Tuckman & Jensen (1977)
Stage 1	**Razzmatazz High** Team members are excited, motivated, optimistic, and determined to succeed.	**Dependency and Inclusion** Team members are dependent on the team leader and concerned about safety and feelings. Motto: The silence of the lambs.	**Searching** Team members are confused over their individual roles and tasks and the team leadership and procedures. Key question: "What are we here for?"	**Forming** Team members do not know each other and are highly anxious. Key task: Establishing trust.
Stage 2	**Grousing** Team members are uncertain about wanting to be in the group. Many complain, and some engage in sabotage.	**Counterdependency and Fight** Team members seek to become less dependent on the team leader and fight among themselves about team goals and procedures. Motto: Wolves in sheep's clothing.	**Defining** Team members define the team tasks, explore their individual roles, and attempt to ascertain their worth within the group. Due to competing agendas, there is conflict among some members. Key question: "What's in it for me?"	**Storming** Team members disagree and clash with each other. Some members form cliques, and some violate team norms. Key task: Managing conflict.

(cont.)

2.1 Four Conceptions of the Stages of Team Development (*cont.*)

	Hills (2001)	Wheelan (1999)	Quick (1992)	Tuckman & Jensen (1977)
Stage 3	**Confusion** Team members decide to work towards the team goal and commit to team spirit, but are unsure how best to achieve these ends. Tasks overlap.	**Trust and Structure** Team members trust one another. They are committed to the team and increasingly willing to cooperate. Motto: How we've changed!	**Identifying** A team feeling arises, and members define their roles in service of the team. Key question: How can we do this better?	**Norming** Team members understand each others expectations more clearly and become more committed to the team. Key task: Focusing on team goals.
Stage 4	**Performing** Everybody knows and understands everyone else. The team is highly productive.	**Work** The team is intensely productive and effective. Motto: In the zone.	**Processing** Team members work together to evaluate their effectiveness. Key question: How well are we doing?	**Performing** The team functions as an integrated unit; support and trust among members is well established. Key task: Looking for new challenges.
Stage 5			**Assimilating/Reforming** The team disbands, completes the tasks at hand, or incorporates new members.	**Mourning** The team "dies" after completing its mission. Key task: Coping and reflecting.

As we can see in Figure 2.1, researchers agree that teams usually go through the following four stages:

- **Stage 1.** Members are uncertain of their roles and their expected level of dependence on team leaders.
- **Stage 2.** Members compete to assert their individuality within the team.
- **Stage 3.** Members renew their commitment to team objectives and develop trust in one another.
- **Stage 4.** Teams achieve their goals by becoming more cohesive and focused on the tasks at hand. They value the individual contributions of members.

We should remember that not all teams will progress through each stage in the same fashion, and some may not even reach the final stage, becoming dysfunctional and unable to achieve their objectives. School culture, leadership styles, and individual personalities can have a profound effect on whether a team succeeds or not.

We know that the stages listed in Figure 2.1 are common for work teams, but are they suitable for teams devoted exclusively to professional development? According to Armstrong and Yarbrough (1996), "Most models of group development stages come from social psychology. Our experience has shown that none of the existing models fully captures the progression necessary for developing internal group environment in learning groups" (p. 35). Instead, the authors contend, learning groups—that is, those devoted to the learning of all group members—progress through five distinct stages.

Stages of Learning Group Development

Stage 1: Politeness. Group members do not express their beliefs or thoughts and focus their efforts on being polite to one another. There is no significant learning at this stage.

Stage 2: Focus. Group members focus increasingly on work planning, negotiating what and how they intend to learn with one another, and sharing their reasons why.

Stage 3: Conflict. Group members clash with one another. Armstrong and Yarbrough explain that these conflicts occur when individuals "struggle to negotiate their place within the group, and the group as a whole struggles to find an identity."

Stage 4: Solidification. The group becomes more cohesive; members begin to understand each other better, and are able to collaborate and learn more easily.

Stage 5: Performance. Groups are productive and highly efficient.

Though these stages clearly overlap with those in Figure 2.1, they are more readily applicable to groups concerned with personal and professional development.

Resolving Team Conflict

If not properly acknowledged, conflicts can pose a serious threat to a team and its aims. According to Quick (1992), conflict

- Is natural,
- Can be resolved through openness,
- Stems from issues rather than personalities,

- Is resolved when we focus on the present, and
- Should be dealt with by the group as a whole.

Conflict can arise when team members hold opposing opinions, when members exhibit characteristics and behaviors that aggravate others, and when the power structure within the team is unequal. Because any of these elements can conspire against group cohesion, group members should be encouraged to view conflict as stemming from issues rather than people.

When managing team conflict, it is important to acknowledge Quick's points and resolve conflict collectively as soon as possible. For example, let's say two team members hold opposing views about the usefulness of certain curriculum materials. Though the members may be tempted to see this conflict as stemming from personal disagreement, the true issue at hand is the usefulness of the materials. Referring colleagues to Quick's suggestions for conflict resolution can help them move past their dispute to focus on the team's goals.

Team Member Roles

According to Meredith Belbin, effective teams are made up of individuals with different but complementary abilities. In her book *Management Teams: Why They Succeed or Fail* (1981), she offers eight general types of team roles based on observed behaviors (see Figure 2.2). It is important to bear in mind that these are generalizations, rather than models to which we should aspire. Not all teams will have members who fit every role, and not every role will exhibit all of the characteristics ascribed to it in Belbin's typology. Every team should map its members' abilities to ensure that the weaknesses of some are balanced by the strengths of others.

2.2 Belbin's Typology of Team Roles

Role	Characteristics
Coordinator	Calm, self-confident, average ability, impartial, enthusiastic
Plant	Individualistic, intellectual, serious, knowledgeable, unorthodox, impractical
Shaper	Active, argumentative, extroverted, impatient, dynamic, provocative
Resource Investigator	Versatile, curious, gregarious, relaxed, extroverted, innovative, communicative
Completer	Persevering, perfectionist, conscientious, detail-oriented, anxious
Monitor	Sober, stoic, discreet, distant, task-oriented, self-centered
Implementer	Disciplined, obstinate, practical, reliable, tolerant, conservative, conscious
Team Worker	Sociable, gregarious, affable, indecisive, responsive, intolerant of conflict

Source: Belbin (1981)

The Four Stages of the Teacher's Choice Framework

The Teacher's Choice Framework delineates four distinct stages of professional development teamwork. By following the guidelines listed for each stage below, educators can get the most out of their collaborative efforts.

Stage 1: Emergence

Once staff members decide to work on their professional development in teams, they should schedule a meeting to share their concerns and chart a professional development plan. At the meeting, each person should make explicit which particular areas of teaching they want to explore further. The time allotted for the inaugural meeting should be generous, with breaks in the discussion. Though many members may feel anxious, they will also be highly motivated.

I have found that a needs-assessment survey (Figure 2.3) can help practitioners disclose their needs and common traits, while also helping them structure their thinking in preparation for a dialogue with colleagues. A preappointed meeting coordinator should be in charge of collecting the completed forms and displaying them around the room. The surveys should be anonymous—one purpose of this exercise is to provide participants with some level of security so that trust building can begin.

When discussing the surveys, team members should look for common themes and areas of concern (beginning with each individual teacher's point of view) and identify sources of expertise, as well as potential team leaders, among the members. Chosen individuals should express their views in response. Team members who are not identified by their peers should be allotted time to reveal their areas of expertise relative to the team's needs. This disclosure of hidden expertise within the school will be the basis for mapping the team's professional development strategy.

The next step is for all team members to report on their students' progress to the group. This can consist simply of a chart showing levels of student performance at intervals over the current or previous academic year (see Figure 2.4). Standardized test results are particularly valuable for this exercise.

The meeting should conclude with participants completing professional development profiles and sharing them with the group (see Figure 2.5). In these preliminary plans for individual development,

2.3 Sample Needs-Assessment Survey

---

1. In 100 words or less, narrate a successful teaching experience that resulted in meaningful student learning.

_____

_____

_____

_____

2. In 100 words or less, narrate a teaching experience that caused you to become concerned about your teaching.

_____

_____

_____

_____

_____

3. Compare the two narratives above. Do you notice any common themes? If so, what are they?

_____

_____

4. Who among your staff could help you with your concerns? Why?

_____

_____

---

members list their personal concerns, which may have changed during the meeting, as well as their areas of expertise and the perceptions they believe other team members have of them. Next they reflect on the three key roles they can play on the team:

- As _peers_, members act as mentors, coresearchers, writing partners, or trainers to their colleagues.
- As _learners_, members focus on improving their own professional practice with the help of one or more peers.
- As _consultants_, members offer support to peer-learner dyads.

2.4 Mr. Griffin's 6th Grade Math Performance Level Chart

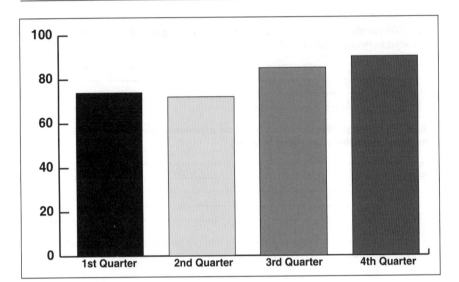

Stage 2: Application

Participants at this stage often feel overwhelmed as they embark on their professional development roles. Team members who find it hard to accept that others think of them as experts, for example, might find self-esteem issues detracting from their motivation. Building administrators or preappointed professional development leaders can be instrumental in helping members at this point—by conferring with them, providing them with resources and other forms of support, helping them to clarify their objectives, or simply listening to what they have to say.

One effective strategy for alleviating anxiety is for each team member to design an individual development plan outlining his or her goals and the steps, resources, activities, and participants needed to achieve them (Figure 2.6).

2.5 Sample Professional Development Profile

Name: _____ Date: _____		
Part 1: Personal Attributes		

Areas of Concern	Areas of Strength	Team Member Perceptions

Part 2: Collaborative Activities

Role	Activity	Advisor for Activity
Peer		
Learner		
Consultant		

2.6 Sample Individual Development Plan

Part 1: Planning

1. Professional Development Goals
List general areas you would like to improve upon:

A.

B.

C.

. . .

2. Learning Objectives
List specific learning objectives tied to the goals above:

A.

B.

C.

. . .

3. Schedule

Month	Week 1	Week 2	Week 3	Week 4
August				
September				
October				
November				
December				
January				
February				
March				
April				
May				
June				
July				

(cont.)

2.6 Sample Individual Development Plan (*cont.*)

4. Budget
Sources of funding:

_____
_____
_____
_____
_____
_____
_____
_____

Proposed expenditure:

_____
_____
_____
_____
_____
_____
_____
_____

5. Expected Student Learning Outcomes

_____
_____
_____
_____
_____
_____
_____
_____

(*cont.*)

2.6 Sample Individual Development Plan (*cont.*)

6. Supporting Activities for Goals and Objectives

Goal A		
Objective A		
Activities	*Fall Semester*	*Spring Semester*

Goal B		
Objective B		
Activities	*Fall Semester*	*Spring Semester*

Goal C		
Objective C		
Activities	*Fall Semester*	*Spring Semester*

(*cont.*)

2.6 Sample Individual Development Plan (*cont.*)

7. Professional Resources at School
Process of identification (How will you select the professional resources you need from those available at school? Who will you ask? What criteria will you use to identify them?):

_____
_____
_____

Names and contact info:

_____
_____
_____

8. Professional Resources in the Community
Process of identification:

_____
_____
_____

Names and contact info:

_____
_____

9. Professional Resources Outside the Community
Process of identification:

_____
_____

Names and contact info:

_____
_____

10. Courses, Seminars, and Conferences
Names, dates held, and contact info:

_____
_____

(*cont.*)

2.6 Sample Individual Development Plan (*cont.*)

Part 2: Self-Evaluation

1. Initial Self-Evaluation
How much do you need to develop in order to reach your goals?

Scale: (1) not at all; (2) a little; (3) a lot

Goal	Date	Rating
A.		
B.		
C.		

2. Self-Evaluation Halfway Through Professional Development Program
How close are you to achieving your goals?

Scale: (1) not at all; (2) a little; (3) a lot

Goal	Date	Rating
A.		
B.		
C.		

3. Self-Evaluation upon Completion of Professional Development Program
How close are you to achieving your goals?

Scale: (1) not at all; (2) a little; (3) a lot

Goal	Date	Rating
A.		
B.		
C.		

In Stage 2, team members engage in what anthropologist Jean Lave (1990) calls "communities of practice." According to Bredo (1997):

> [Communities of practice are] a way of emphasizing, first, that in learning as apprenticeship, one's social role is also changing as a part of learning. For instance, one may begin as a peripheral participant and move toward involvement in more central aspects of the activity, changing roles as one goes. Second, one is a "participant" or cocreator of the activity. Whatever activity is going on will ultimately be a joint product, not something determined by only one party. Finally, most learning that is of any importance occurs as a result of participation in the practical activities of a *community*. Learning is about becoming a full-fledged member of a community rather than simply performing an isolated task. (pp. 37–38)

Stage 3: Appropriation

In the third stage, participants become aware of their own development and the work it takes to incorporate new knowledge into their teaching repertoire. Participants arguably learn the most in this stage, during which they begin to question their work methods and experiment with new ideas. By folding new knowledge into practice they pick and choose whatever concepts and applications are best-suited to individual classroom conditions.

Though rewarding, this stage can confuse participants who operate at different levels simultaneously. It can be difficult for team members to become more self-aware while at the same time helping colleagues to do so. In a sense, participants who work simultaneously as experts and novices experience a sort of "double consciousness" (Du Bois, 1953), and may feel pressured by having to attend to the work of both stages at the same time. Administrators should therefore help team members ask themselves what they are doing and why. Answering these two simple questions can help participants keep their professional development plans in line with the school's needs as well as their own.

Stage 4: Transformation

By the fourth and final stage, participants have begun to engage in learning as an activity concerned as much with improving the school as a whole as with equipping them with knowledge. Skills gained through professional development constitute new intellectual capital for the school, and as such empower everyone. Professional development teaches participants to be team members (and more importantly, community members), and transforms their views on teaching and student learning. This last dimension dovetails with Bereiter's (2002) idea of educational progress as the construction of intellectual artifacts—highly situated theories or ideas that affect the totality of an organization and enhance the intellectual wealth of the profession. This stage is comparable to Hills's (2001) "Performing" stage and Wheelan's (1999) "Work" stage, and should be relatively short so that the team can turn to new challenges, or begin incorporating new members.

Upon achieving individual and team goals, the team will go through a process akin to Quick's (1992) "Assimilating/Reforming" stage or Tuckman and Jensen's (1977) "Mourning" stage. They may "mourn" the passing of the previous stage nostalgia for "the good old days"—and team members may revert to old practices—but given the momentum attained in development, the new knowledge will

hopefully become integrated into the school culture. Though participants may break bonds with some team partners on specific professional development activities—for example, by terminating a
mentoring relationship—they will build new ones with others outside
the team (as in the case of collaborative action research). Likewise,
lessons learned during professional development can be renewed and
made more effective by communicating them to the broader educational community: teachers may choose to write journal articles,
develop new curriculum materials, run in-service courses and seminars,
or present at professional conferences, to name just a few examples.

– 3 –

Mentoring

A mentor is merely a more seasoned pupil, further along the journey. A mentee holds within himself the seeds of a future mentor.
—*I Ching* (Frid, 1994, p. 247)

Cindy's Story

Cindy works as a reading specialist at a youth center in a big U.S. city. She is devoted to her work with at-risk youth, having herself lost a child to drugs a few years earlier. Cindy is a model practitioner: she keeps up-to-date by attending workshops and conferences, reads extensively in the field, and implements cutting-edge practices.

This was not the case three years ago. At that time she was teaching along the same old path and felt unable to cope with the day-to-day chores of her job. She had completed her graduate studies ten years earlier, and though she knew she possessed the knowledge necessary for working at the youth center, she was frequently depressed by the stories her students brought to class and felt unable to address their many special needs. After almost 18 years in the profession, she was considering dropping out.

Cindy simply endured the stress of her job until she met Terry, a Spanish teacher in the center's charter middle school. An immigrant herself, Terry had lived in the neighborhood ever since she arrived in the United States. She and Cindy met by chance in the staff room one Friday afternoon and started talking over coffee about their respective challenges. It was apparent to Cindy that Terry had a zest for knowledge and an acute perception of her students' lives. Cindy also learned about Terry's many success stories, which reinforced Cindy's own sense of inadequacy. For almost two hours, Terry helped Cindy brainstorm ways to improve her teaching—beginning a professional dialogue that would ultimately last three years.

Two weeks after their initial meeting, the principal of the center asked Terry to serve as a mentor for Cindy and reflect on Cindy's need to explore successful classroom practices. In the course of one year, Terry and Cindy met once a week. They wrote about their work with students, visited each other's classes, developed a research project on practices best suited to their students, and together developed a research-based dual-language reading curriculum for the middle school.

After two years of collaborating, Cindy had discovered her hidden teaching talents and was on a steep learning curve. Terry, in turn, had learned a lot about how personal circumstances can limit our perceptions. She discovered just how hard it had been for Cindy to concentrate on her work after the death of her son, as well as the impact this tragedy had had on Cindy's classroom performance. She also learned about Cindy's expertise as a reading instructor, and adapted many of her ideas for use with her own students. By the end of their three-year collaboration, both teachers had not only grown personally and professionally, but also given their students more opportunities.

Defining the Process

Mentoring in education has gained considerable momentum over the past fifteen years. It quickly became widely used as a model for induction, especially during a teacher's first year of practice. As Hale (1999) explains, "Many organizations are turning to mentoring as a way of supporting the continuing professional development of managers, often relying on little more than common sense and anecdotal evidence in setting up mentoring initiatives."

According to Fletcher (2000), mentoring "reflects the potential of a one-to-one professional relationship that can simultaneously empower and enhance practice. . . . Mentoring should unblock the ways to change by building self-esteem, self-confidence and a readiness to act as well as to engage in constructive interpersonal relations." As Carruthers (1993) notes, "there is evidence that formally arranged mentoring programs do very much better than any other. . . . Mentors are influential people who significantly help you reach your major life goals." However, because mentor as well as mentee must scrutinize and reflect on one another's attitudes, beliefs, and behaviors while simultaneously building trust and respect, the process can be difficult for many.

Lunt, Bennett, McKenzie, and Powell (1992); Tomlinson (1998); English (1999); Parsloe and Wray (2000); and Fletcher (2000) all point out that sustained involvement in mentoring provides teachers with increased opportunities for honing their skills in support of instructional change. However, this can only occur if the mentoring process is separated from contractual evaluation or other forms of institutional appraisal (Costa & Garmston, 2002).

Teachers often confuse mentoring with tutoring, but they are two different processes. Tutors work according to an agenda of prespecified goals, transmitting their knowledge to the learner in top-down fashion, as a teacher would to a student. Mentoring, on the other hand, is a process of mutual growth, during which mentor and mentee engage in cycles of active learning that result in enhancement of practice and empowerment of those involved. Put simply, tutoring is done *to* learners, whereas mentoring is done *with* them.

According to Tomlinson (1998), "the basic functions of mentoring are to actively assist mentees with:

- Acquisition of awareness and strategies relevant to teaching
- Engagement in teaching activity which deploys such strategies and awareness
- Monitoring of these teaching activities and their effects
- Adapting strategy and awareness in the light of reflection on such feedback
- Motivation and the harnessing of their personal strengths through appropriate interpersonal strategies and awareness." (p. 20)

Whitmore (cited in Parsloe & Wray, 2000) considers the following to be the "essential mental qualities" (p. 130) necessary for engaging in mentoring:

- **Responsibility.** Taking personal responsibility for both success and failure.
- **Awareness.** Focusing on what is going on around one while one is performing.
- **Concentration.** Remaining in a passive state while focusing on the task.
- **Relaxation.** Keeping anxiousness out by focusing on the here and now.

- **Detachment.** Standing apart mentally from the activity so as to observe it and its actions.
- **Commitment.** The will to achieve through honest effort.
- **Trust.** Being fully prepared we can trust our own mind and body to reproduce the action or task.

Clearly, mentoring involves more than informal consultation between colleagues. For one thing, mentoring—if structured with a view toward the holistic development of both mentor and mentee—has a more lasting effect than do less formal relationships, which usually address short-term issues and tend to break up once those issues are resolved. For holistic development to take root, time and resources need to be allotted both by school and district administrators.

Mentoring is a social-constructivist endeavor. As Wertsch (1999) notes:

> Cognition does not reside in the minds of individuals. In any teaching encounter, the teacher must represent his/her learners' mind in his own mind. In turn, learners must recreate the teacher's mind in their own. Thus, it is through the interchange of ideas that cognition is constructed. Not in the minds of the individuals, but in the possibilities for interaction. (pp. 40–41)

Choosing a Mentor

Just as not everyone is suited to teaching, not every teacher should become a mentor. Though selection procedures for mentoring will vary, they need to be carefully considered; proper qualifications should be recognized as critical to the success of the program. Fletcher (2000) suggests that teachers "should bring to mentoring a willingness to listen and to support but not an overwhelming drive to solve others' problems."

I would add that they should also be able to critique their mentees' development in an empathetic but truthful manner. All too often, mentors find it hard to challenge mentees. However, it is in their ability to be both counselors and challengers that the mentors' roles will make sense.

One of the first things prospective mentors should do is reflect on their willingness to engage in the process. Experience shows that the efficacy of mentors is proportional to their readiness for the task. Figure 3.1 shows a sample questionnaire that can be used to involve mentoring candidates in reflection.

Once a teacher decides to become a mentor, he or she must develop a "mentor mindset"—what Millwater and Yarrow (1997) refer to as "the holistic structure of attitudes, values, and beliefs about teaching and learning through which professional knowledge is filtered and from which action/practice issues."

Mentors should model professional thinking and decision-making processes that allow for the fine-tuning of teaching and learning for their mentees. In order to do this, mentors will most likely have to open up their own practice to the scrutiny of their mentees. As Fletcher (2000) notes, "It is ironic that we spend years learning how to make our teaching implicit. . . . [when] as mentors we have to unpack what we do and why for sharing. Before we can share what we do we need to be able to know what we are doing—to make the implicit things we do explicit." To learn how to "make the implicit things we do explicit," prospective mentors should take a preparation course (see Figure 3.2 for a sample course schedule).

Ideally, preparation courses should be taught by seasoned mentors—teachers with broad experience developing mentoring relationships in a

3.1 Sample Reflection Questionnaire for Prospective Mentors

Please answer the following questions:

- What can you contribute to the professional development of a mentee?
- What skills do you possess that will help you interact with a mentee?
- What skills do you still need in order to fully participate in mentoring?
- Are you adequately prepared to provide a mentee with feedback and guidance?
- Are you willing to share specifics about your own practice with a mentee?
- Are you ready to nurture as well as challenge a mentee?
- Do you understand that mentoring is a two-way process?
- Are you willing to face the challenges of mentoring?
- What are your teaching strengths? How can you best communicate them to a mentee?
- What are your teaching weaknesses? How can you improve them?
- What do you expect to gain from the mentoring relationship?

variety of contexts. Courses benefit from the presence of the principal and assistant principal, who may dwell more deeply on the organizational dimension of mentoring (for example, by addressing budgeting and scheduling issues). Though course length may vary, two days are enough to accommodate the minimum requirements for a thorough introduction to the topic.

Mentoring Models

Many authors agree that mentoring, like the teams discussed in Chapter 2, consists of stages (Brooks & Sikes, 1997; Fletcher, 2000; Hawkey, 1997; Tomlinson, 1998). By structuring the mentoring

3.2 Sample Mentor Preparation Course Schedule

Day 1
A.M.: Understanding Mentoring
Issues covered include:

- Roles, relationships, and processes
- Differences between mentoring and tutoring
- The need for structured mentoring
- Mentor reflection questionnaire

P.M.: Mentee Development
Covers career stages and mentoring models.

Day 2
A.M.: Essential Mentoring Skills I
Covers trust and confidence building and the importance of communication.

P.M.: Essential Mentoring Skills II
Covers the mentor's roles as model, support, critic, and evaluator.

Day 3
A.M.: Essential Mentoring Skills III
Issues covered include:

- How to observe and respond to teaching
- Different approaches to classroom observation
- Clinical supervision-based approaches

P.M.: Essential Mentoring Skills IV
Issues covered include:

- Challenging mentees
- Providing feedback and promoting reflection
- Developing the mentoring relationship

process accordingly, participants can ensure a methodological experience. Fletcher (2000) discusses the following five stages, based on Furlong and Maynard's characterization of the stages novice teachers go through during mentoring:

Stage 1: Idealism. Mentees have an overly simplistic view of teaching and learning, concentrating on their teaching and on being liked by students while overlooking the importance of learning itself.

Stage 2: Survival. Mentees tend to be reactive rather than proactive, focusing on emergent classroom issues but unable to anticipate them.

Stage 3: Coping. Mentees tend to replicate what they believe to be appropriate behavior, mimicking their own idealized models of good teaching and imitating other educators, without knowing the reasons those educators acted the way they did.

Stage 4: Hitting the Plateau. Mentees show little appreciation of how teaching affects learning. They tend to stick to the lesson plan and use whatever teaching techniques have worked well for them so far, disregarding other potential courses of action.

Stage 5: Moving On. Mentees begin to center their efforts on improving student learning.

As with any model, there are exceptions to the stages listed above, and individuals may not move along the stages in a linear way. These stages represent possible paths mentees may take during induction or mentoring, but the steps need not be sequential. Interestingly, the mentor will also progress through approximately the same stages as the mentee.

The Craft Model

According to Brooks and Sikes (1997), the "craft model" of mentoring is best for approaching stages 1 and 2 of the process, as it allows mentees to serve as apprentices to their mentors, watching and learning from the mentor's practice. The inherent danger of this model is that mentees can become little more than clones of their mentors. Still, purposeful observation of exemplary practices helps mentees learn how to perform at higher levels of expertise, and increases their awareness of key factors influencing their teaching.

The Competency-Based Model

The competency-based model of mentoring, in which mentees work on discrete teaching competencies, works particularly well in Stage 3. But competencies can be either a liberating or a stifling point of departure: if they are taken as proof of development, then they are nothing more than models to emulate; if, on the other hand, they are taken as indicators of a path the mentee should follow, then they can be very empowering. Still, mentees are likely to become frustrated if they are unable to attain certain levels of competence, thus leading them to plateau. In such a situation, both mentor and mentee should engage in sustained reflection on what aspects of practice the mentee should work on, as well as on how best the mentor can support this exploration.

The Reflective Model

The reflective model of mentoring helps mentees move on after hitting a plateau in Stage 4. Reflection can take a while, so mentors should ensure that they schedule enough time for it. Proper reflection can lead teachers to develop their own "living theories" about practice in the classroom (Whitehead, 2001). Teachers who do not engage in appropriate reflection may work to improve specific competencies or emulate a model teacher, but fail to develop their own individual philosophies of teaching.

Figure 3.3 shows the relationships between the stages of mentee development, the learning that occurs at each stage, and the mentoring model appropriate for each.

3.3 Mentoring Stages and Models

Mentoring Stage	Type of Learning	Appropriate Model
1. Idealism	"Learning to see"	Craft model
2. Survival		
3. Coping	"Learning to do"	Competency model
4. Hitting the Plateau		
5. Moving On	"Learning to be"	Reflective model

Reflection cannot and should not be relegated to the end stages of a mentoring relationship. Mentors as well as mentees should recursively search their experiences and actions for clues about how to improve their skills. This process is known as "intellectual reflection," and is similar to Schön's (1983) idea of reflection on action. When reflection is closely followed by action on the part of the mentor, the mentee, or both, the combination becomes a form of practice. For example, after observing the mentee at work, a mentor may decide that the mentee's criteria observation were not adequate given the aims of the lesson. As a result of this reflection, the mentor may choose to repeat the observation using a more fitting approach.

Mentoring works best when the mentor is at Level 1 in the Teacher's Choice Framework and the mentee is at Level 3 or 4 (see Figure 1.3 in Chapter 1). In other words, the process works best as a form of support for colleagues who are aware of their learning needs, though it can prove effective with others as well.

In order for mentoring to succeed, evaluation should be separated from the professional development process. When mentors are in charge of evaluation, the pressure on the mentees to do well can undermine their trust and confidence. Because the true purpose of mentoring is to help the novice develop and scaffold her learning, both mentor and mentee should focus more on process than on outcomes. If mentors are required to evaluate mentees, the fundamental trust-building component of their relationship may be undermined. The balance of power should never shift too heavily toward the mentor, disempowering the mentee. At all times, the mentor should be more of a "guide on the side" than a "sage on the stage."

– 4 –

Collaborative Action Research

Speed bumps: raised places in the road that limit one's speed. When we are moving too fast, we must suddenly slow down or be thrown off course.

—Weis and Fine (2000, p. 1)

The Dilemma of Keystone High School

John, Kathy, Alison, and Brad have worked at Keystone High School for the past six years. At a faculty meeting last year, they were surprised to find that a particularly difficult group of 11th graders showed consistent signs of underachievement in all subjects. The four staff members worked with most of the students in that group, and did not understand why they were faring so poorly when other students, exposed to the same teaching methods, seemed to be succeeding.

Together, the four decided to explore the issue in depth. John, a counselor, reviewed the students' files for information about their backgrounds and their previous learning experiences, and interviewed the students as well as some of their former teachers. In her math class, Kathy monitored the participation of students from the under-achieving group, creating a chart that indicated when and how each of the students participated. She shared this chart with Brad, who taught science, and soon they noticed that underachieving students exhibited similar behavioral patterns in both their classes.

For her part, Alison, an English teacher, experimented with alter-native grouping of the underachievers in her class, making sure that each of the students under observation was assigned to a different, heterogeneous group. She found that the students seemed to respond better to such grouping.

When the four colleagues discussed the students, Alison, Kathy, and Brad were surprised by what John had discovered: all of the stu-dents came from single-parent homes and had a history of under-achievement and relational problems. The teachers decided to review the literature on working with at-risk students and agreed to collabo-rate on improving the students' achievement.

Following their review of the research, the teachers agreed to con-sistently apply a set of teaching procedures in their classes and moni-tor the students' progress for three weeks. When they reconvened, results were mixed: though Alison's students were making steady progress, Brad's and Kathy's were not. The four decided to split into two pairs to further research the issue. In addition, John recruited three other teachers to use the same techniques as Alison, Brad, and Kathy and monitor student progress.

After another three weeks, the group got together again and dis-cussed which techniques they had found particularly suitable for their students. It soon became evident that one particular activity—Think-Pair-Share—had proved useful for students in all classes. As a result, the group set out to find ways of involving the students in activities similar to Think-Pair-Share.

By the end of the ninth week of collaboration, the four educators, along with the colleagues John brought aboard, had developed a set of best practices specifically suited to the students they were monitoring. The group agreed to disseminate its findings and to systematically apply the best practices in their classes. Toward the end of the semester, underachieving students were making steady progress in most subjects, even if they were not all performing at grade level.

Collective vs. Individual Action Research

Johnson (1993) defines action research as "a deliberate, solution-oriented investigation that is group or personally owned and conducted. It is characterized by spiraling cycles of problem identification, systematic data collection, reflection, analysis, data-driven action taken, and, finally, problem redefinition" (p. 1). As Fletcher (2000) points out, "Before we can share what we do we need to be able to know what we are doing—to make the implicit things we do explicit—and research can help us understand what we do so we can share" (p. 49). Action research carried out in classrooms by teachers has the potential to increase awareness about teaching and learning, and to enhance conditions in both areas. Unfortunately much of the literature about this approach focuses on the individual efforts of isolated teachers. Because solitary action research serves to further a culture of isolation, it is my view that the practice should be conducted in collaboration with colleagues.

By probing into their everyday realities and actions, educators can discover a world of meanings and routines that have the potential to harm or benefit student learning. The dialogue that follows such a discovery forms the basis for a situated theory of learning and teaching tailored to the particular needs of students and teachers at the school. As Reason (1994) points out, "It is through dialogue that the subject-object relationship of traditional science gives way to a subject-subject one, in which the academic knowledge of formally educated people works in a dialectical tension with the popular knowledge of the people to produce a more profound understanding of the situation." Collaborative action research, notes Reason, has two objectives: "One aim is to produce knowledge and action directly useful to a group of people—through research, adult education, and sociopolitical action. The second aim is to empower people at a second and deeper level through the process of constructing and using their own knowledge" (p. 328).

Much of the literature on action research focuses on actions that leave both students and teachers at the margin of the inquiry process. In my view, individual action research reinforces the subject-object paradigm alluded to above by Reason, so that the school culture and climate remain mostly unchanged. By contrast, an approach to research that focuses on collective inquiry that is relevant to as wide an audience as possible can help direct improvement efforts to the actual needs of the community, rather than just to one of its members. By paying direct attention to problems stemming from daily practice, collaborative action research acknowledges and values the teachers' living theories as sources of knowledge, leading to both personal and social change. As Tandon (cited in Reason, 1994) notes:

[Collaborative action research] values the people's knowledge, sharpens their capacity to conduct their own research in their own interest, helps them appropriate knowledge produced by the dominant knowledge industry for their own interests and purposes, allows problems to be explored from their perspective, and, maybe most important, liberates their minds for critical reflection, questioning, and the continuous pursuit of inquiry thus contributing to the liberation of their minds and the development of freedom and democracy. (p. 329)

Collaborative Action Research: The Process

The process of collaborative action research starts with a strong focus on action (Cohen & Manion, 2000). The main area of study should be the situation of the community as a whole, and not just of discrete members, though the initial trigger for reflection may be a specific classroom occurrence. McTaggart (1997) explains this process as follows:

> In deciding just where to begin in making improvements, a group identifies an area where members perceive a cluster of problems of mutual concern and consequence. The group decides to work together on a 'thematic concern.' . . . Put simply, [this kind of classroom] research is the way in which groups of people can organize the conditions under which they can learn from their own experience and make this experience accessible to others. (p. 27)

Though action research is often depicted as a spiral of reflection and action, it is not far from positivist prescriptions that might curb practitioner freedom, thus narrowing the scope of inquiry. Many teachers who claim to engage in action research are actually using a linear set of prescribed steps to investigate matters of concern (O'Brien, 1998).

In her 1999 book *Decolonizing Methodologies*, Linda Tuhiwai Smith presents an alternative to the traditional action research process that might be beneficial to teachers. In contrast with traditional action research, which is linear and cyclical, Tuhiwai Smith's conception of collaborative research focuses on the learning community as a collective whose actions stem from community needs, of which there are the three following types:

1. **Maintenance.** Needs related to the school's day-to-day reality (e.g., aligning standards with teaching practices that are effective with a certain group of students).
2. **Recovery.** Needs related to remediation (e.g., improving student performance on tests).
3. **Development.** Needs related to enhancing school assets (e.g., adopting a curriculum development framework).

Seen from this perspective, action research becomes a community-empowerment tool. Tuhiwai Smith suggests that actions stemming from research need to meet the needs of the community, since they will inevitably affect the way the community understands, mobilizes, transforms, and improves itself. By meeting these needs, educators reconfigure the school community as a whole—contributing to the power of collaborative action research.

The Six Steps of Collaborative Action Research

Educators who engage in collaborative action research are committed to examining their practice in order to enhance student learning. To succeed, they must have a heightened awareness of their own actions and those of their peers to discern community needs. This self-aware inquiry process has six distinct steps:

- Posing unambiguous questions
- Charting the inquiry
- Gathering relevant data
- Interpreting the data
- Taking action
- Reflecting on the consequences of the action

These steps do not necessarily occur in sequence, nor are they intended to be followed at all costs. Data gathered to address a particular question may itself raise additional concerns, as may actions taken to address a question. The steps are intended more as awareness milestones: junctures during the collaborative research process at which practitioners might stop to reflect on the problems posed. These are the "speed bumps" Weis and Fine refer to in the quote at the beginning of this chapter. Because the research can change directions in between these junctures, flexibility among practitioners is particularly important.

Step 1: Posing Unambiguous Questions

Questions to address during collaborative research can be far ranging. Participants might conduct an inquiry into issues relating to the curriculum, student learning, their own teaching practice, their characteristics as teachers, the school as a whole, and many other areas of interest. It is vital, however, that the group reach consensus about the issue at stake before embarking on any inquiry. It's also important to avoid jargon by wording the questions in everyday terms, as well as to narrow the focus of inquiry as much as possible. Clarity of language and purpose helps all members of the learning community to better perceive the issue at stake and the steps to be undertaken. Well-developed questions help practitioners to select relevant data sources and gathering techniques, and provide them with a framework for data interpretation. A good question allows teachers to revisit the situation that generated the inquiry by providing them with recurrent approximations of the matter from different perspectives. The variety of viewpoints allows practitioners to probe deeper into their understanding of the issues raised—as well as the possible solutions. Figure 4.1 provides a template to help educators construct effective questions for collaborative action research.

Charting the Inquiry

A graphic representation of the inquiry process can add clarity of purpose to action research, and has certain advantages over verbal descriptions in that it

- Provides a common focus of information to all participants.
- Clarifies the path of the inquiry.
- Makes verbal information explicit.
- Portrays relationships and connections among issues and actions.
- Reveals the systemic nature of the inquiry in an easily visualized representation.
- Offers a model for thinking about the issue at stake.
- Helps identify sources and means for action.

Graphic representations can take many forms; it is the community's responsibility to decide on the best possible representation given its purposes in developing the inquiry. As long as the representation is

4.1 Asking the Right Question

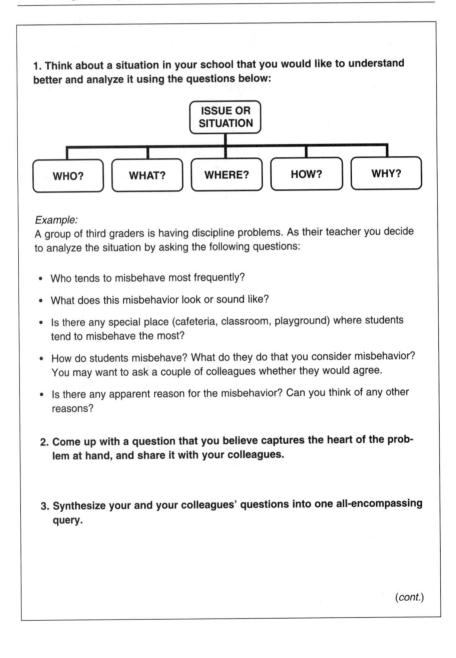

1. Think about a situation in your school that you would like to understand better and analyze it using the questions below:

Example:
A group of third graders is having discipline problems. As their teacher you decide to analyze the situation by asking the following questions:

- Who tends to misbehave most frequently?

- What does this misbehavior look or sound like?

- Is there any special place (cafeteria, classroom, playground) where students tend to misbehave the most?

- How do students misbehave? What do they do that you consider misbehavior? You may want to ask a couple of colleagues whether they would agree.

- Is there any apparent reason for the misbehavior? Can you think of any other reasons?

2. Come up with a question that you believe captures the heart of the problem at hand, and share it with your colleagues.

3. Synthesize your and your colleagues' questions into one all-encompassing query.

(cont.)

4.1 Asking the Right Question (*cont.*)

---

4. Using the following checklist, assess the suitability of the synthesis question. If the question does not meet all of the criteria listed, return to Step 1 above.

Is the question related to the issue at hand?	YES	NO
Is the issue a real concern for everyone in the group?	YES	NO
Are there sufficient data to develop an inquiry on the issue?	YES	NO
Can data be gathered in the context of your daily duties?	YES	NO
Can data be interpreted without access to sophisticated technology?	YES	NO
Are potential answers to the question easy to communicate?	YES	NO

---

clear to all practitioners and hews to the focus and spirit of the inquiry, it will be useful. Whatever form it takes, the graphic should also be able to change to accommodate shifts in the research process.

Figure 4.2 shows sample graphics that can be used to chart collaborative action research projects. As you can see, simplicity of presentation is a key factor in these representations. Though I have included two types of charts, a single one per inquiry is best. In the figure, you will notice that the second example is not as explicit as the first; this is something to consider when choosing a type of graphic. The more explicit the diagram, the clearer it will be for all those involved. Detailed diagrams are also more helpful research tools and more engaging to readers. In addition to the examples presented here, Venn diagrams, flowcharts, scatterplots, and tree diagrams are other options for charting an inquiry.

4.2 Graphic Representation Examples for Collaborative Action Research

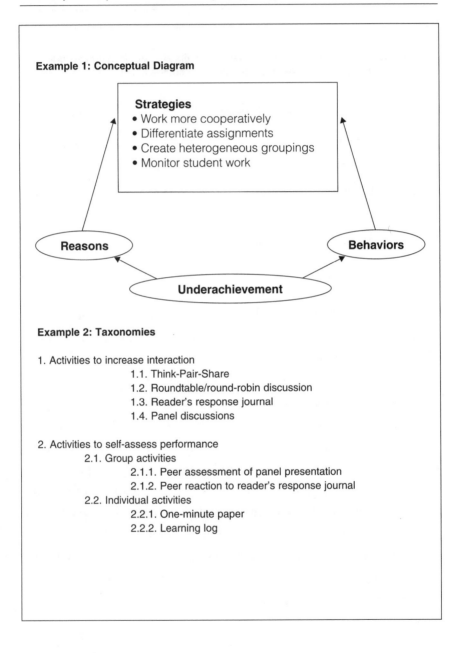

Example 1: Conceptual Diagram

Strategies
- Work more cooperatively
- Differentiate assignments
- Create heterogeneous groupings
- Monitor student work

Reasons

Behaviors

Underachievement

Example 2: Taxonomies

1. Activities to increase interaction
       1.1. Think-Pair-Share
       1.2. Roundtable/round-robin discussion
       1.3. Reader's response journal
       1.4. Panel discussions

2. Activities to self-assess performance
     2.1. Group activities
       2.1.1. Peer assessment of panel presentation
       2.1.2. Peer reaction to reader's response journal
     2.2. Individual activities
       2.2.1. One-minute paper
       2.2.2. Learning log

Gathering Relevant Data

In order to make sure the data are reliable and valid, they must be gathered systematically over time and focused on the aim of the inquiry. There are many possible sources of data, and just as many ways of collecting them. Of course, the data to be gathered will depend on the focus of the inquiry. Practitioners should be particularly vigilant of how they store their data: because classroom events are ephemeral and cannot be duplicated, it is advisable to record relevant experiences as soon as they happen and to keep the document for future reference.

Le Compte and Schensul (1999) describe three processes for data gathering:

- **Inscription.** The process of making mental notes.
- **Description.** The process of communicating mental notes through writing.
- **Transcription.** The process of quoting directly in writing.

Different types of data can be gathered at different times using different means. What is crucial is that the data be promptly recorded to allow for analysis.

According to Le Compte and Schensul (1999), "Ethnographers have only three basic kinds of data: information about what people say, what they do, and what they leave behind in the form of manufactured artifacts and documents." As ethnographers of their schools' cultures, collaborative action researchers have the same kinds of data at their disposal. Figure 4.3 shows a list of different possible data sources for selected foci of inquiry.

4.3 Possible Sources of Data for Collaborative Action Research

Focus of Inquiry	Possible Data Sources
Students	• Samples of student work • Grades • Interviews • Focused observation • Checklists • Surveys • Teacher-student correspondence • Tests
Curriculum	• Curriculum guides • Syllabi • Curriculum documents • State or district mandates • Samples of student work • Samples of teacher work
Teaching	• Observation • Lesson or unit plans • Tasks or activities created for classroom use • Professional development portfolios • Interviews • Surveys • Journals or diaries • Student grades • Curriculum documents created by teacher
School	• Timetables • Observation • Interviews • School documents • Student schedules • Teacher schedules • Non-teaching staff schedules • Facilities and equipment
School-community relations	• Observation • Surveys • Hours of community involvement in school • Hours of school involvement in community • Interviews • Communications

Interpreting Data, Taking Action, and Reflecting on Action

When interpreting data, practitioners draw conclusions that will further their inquiry by suggesting the next steps to take. The processes of interpreting data, taking action, and reflecting on action are interdependent: though not sequentially organized, they feed back on one another in dialectical interaction.

Practitioners analyze data through various filters, such as their personal and professional experiences, level of knowledge, and individual and community core values. Interpretation must therefore be collaborative, since the greater the number of perspectives, the more targeted and effective the inquiry will be.

Researchers should reflect on data both before and after taking action on them. Griffiths and Tann (1992) suggest that there are five different dimensions to reflection:

- **Rapid.** Occurs immediately and automatically during an action; similar to Schön's (1983) notion of reflection-in-action.
- **Repair.** Occurs during a pause in action.
- **Review.** Occurs after action as a recap of events; best as a collaborative effort.
- **Research.** Methodical and focused around particular issues.
- **Retheorizing.** Educators contrast their own theories—gained through experience—with those from other practitioners, including academics. This is the most rigorous type of reflection.

Zeichner and Liston (1996) contend that "teachers need to reflect within all of these dimensions at one time or another and that too much of a focus on particular dimensions to the neglect of the others will lead to superficial reflection in which teachers' practical theories and practices are not questioned" (p. 47).

When engaging in reflection as proposed by Zeichner and Liston, educators should ask themselves the following questions:

- Why am I doing this?
- Why am I doing it this way and not another way?
- Is there a different way of doing this?
- How can a different way of doing this help me?
  - o How can it help my learners?
  - o How can it help my community?
- Why would I choose to do things differently? (Nolan & Hoover, in press)

Though there may not be any ready answers to these questions, the questions alone can help provide perspective.

Communicating

It is very important that those involved in collaborative action research communicate their insights to the wider community. The purpose of communication is twofold: to let practitioners clarify the goals and actions of the inquiry, and to validate their activities in the eyes of others. As McTaggart explains:

Validation in participatory action research is accomplished by a variety of methods, particularly those reported in methodological literature of interpretive inquiry and including the triangulation of observations and interpretations, by establishing credibility among participants and informants, by participant confirmation, by the deliberate establishment of an "audit trail" of data and interpreta-tions, and by testing the coherence of arguments being presented in a "critical community" or a community of "critical friends" whose commitment is to testing the arguments and evidence advanced in the account of the study. This is typically an extended process of iteration between the data, the literature that informs the study (substantively and methodologically), participants in the study, and critical friends and others who have an informed interest in the study. That is, validation is an explicit process of dialogue, it is not achieved by adherence to a fixed procedure. (1997, p. 13)

Communication can occur at different times, through different means, and for different purposes; it is not necessarily a final product of the inquiry. It can help researchers better understand themselves, their peers, and the issue at hand; mobilize practitioners at the class-room, school, community, and district level; transform a school's cul-ture, climate, and reputation in the community; and reveal improvements in teaching and learning.

Collaborative Action Research and the Teacher's Choice Framework

As a professional development strategy embedded in the daily activi-ties of educators, collaborative action research allows practitioners to tap the internal resources of their school while also providing a forum for reflection on improvement. Because it capitalizes on educators' awareness of development needs, collaborative action research is a Level 3 activity in the Teacher's Choice Framework. The process can affect other development activities too: insights gained through action research can be transformed into field notes (see Chapter 6), for instance, and practitioners can use their newfound knowledge for in-house teacher training. As with the other professional development activities in the Teacher's Choice Framework, collaborative action research benefits from being both community-based and iterative in nature.

– 5 –

Peer Coaching

The word mediate is derived from the word "middle." Therefore, mediators interpose themselves between a person and some event, problem, conflict, challenge or other perplexing situation. The mediator intervenes in such a way as to enhance another person's self-directed learning.

—Costa and Garmston (2002, p. 56)

Paul and Meghan

Paul has taught 3rd grade in a small suburban school since 1990 and feels very comfortable with that grade level. For the past year, he has tried to implement a new curriculum model in his classes. He attended a two-day workshop at the local intermediate unit, conducted extensive bibliographical and Internet research on the model, and designed mini-units for use in his class.

Despite all this he was not confident that his efforts were effective, so one day he asked a fellow 3rd grade teacher, Meghan, to sit in on Mone of his classes. Prior to class, Paul explained the new curriculum model to Meghan and asked her to observe the level of student involvement in different activities. When class began, Meghan took copious notes on student involvement and gave them to Paul for analysis.

After analyzing the data, Paul concluded that he had to drastically alter his teaching approach if he really wanted his students to learn; the data showed that the new curriculum model was certainly no guarantee of increased achievement. So he made changes to his original plan and asked Meghan to repeat her classroom observation and assess the effectiveness of his restructured model. After class, the two teachers discussed the experience and planned further alterations to the framework to better serve Paul's students.

By now, Meghan had grown curious about Paul's curriculum model and asked him to help her apply it to her own classroom. During the second semester, Meghan and Paul switched places: she started using the framework in her class and he sat in on her lessons, guiding her application of the model. Together they reflected on how this theoretical framework could best be adapted to the reality of their school and their students.

At a recent staff meeting, Paul and Meghan communicated their findings to the rest of the faculty. They discovered that a 2nd grade teacher was also trying to implement the same framework in her class, and decided that the three of them should visit each other's classes to vary their perspectives. Since then, student achievement has increased in both the 2nd and 3rd grades, and the school principal has asked Paul, Meghan, and the 2nd grade teacher to coach their colleagues in implementing the curriculum model.

Peer Coaching

Paul and Meghan's activities in the story above are generally known as "peer coaching." According to Galbraith and Anstrom (1991),

> Peer coaching is defined as a professional development method that has been shown to increase collegiality and improve teaching. It is a confidential process through which teachers share their expertise and provide one another with feedback, support, and assistance for the purpose of refining present skills, learning new skills, and/or solving classroom-related problems. Peer coaching also refers to in-class training by a supportive peer who helps the teacher apply skills learned in a workshop. Coached teachers experience significant positive changes in their behaviors, when provided with an appropriate program that ensures accountability, support, companionship, and specific feedback over an extended period of time. (p. 1)

This approach has become increasingly popular over the past two decades, particularly through the work of Beverly Showers (1982). Originally, peer coaching was intended as a follow-up to traditional training, and had three distinct stages: a clinical assessment of a teacher's skill and readiness level, training in a specific method that the teacher should apply in classes, and classroom observations to confirm that the teacher is integrating the model into his or her lessons. A similar process applied to coaches: first their coaching skills would be assessed, then they would receive training on how to coach, and then they would be observed in action by more experienced coaches. In both instances, the three-stage process is nominally cyclical, and can be repeated indefinitely until the teachers or coaches have perfected their tasks. (For a visual depiction of the process, see Figure 5.1.)

5.1 Diagram of the Traditional Three-Stage Peer-Coaching Cycle

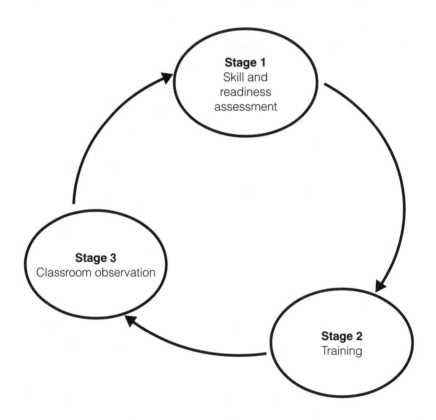

I would suggest a departure from the conventional approach to peer coaching, which reinforces an outmoded view of supervision and professional development by adhering to a transmission model. In the traditional view, the coach is the expert who "transmits" expertise

to the novice while at the same time evaluating the novice's performance on prescribed skills. It also supports the idea that teachers need to be fixed, leaving little room for a modality of teacher growth centered on teachers' needs.

Paul and Meghan shared power equally, and their relationship was initiated by both of them for the purpose of their mutual education. In peer coaching, all participants are empowered because everyone's needs are attended to and they build shared knowledge that is directly relevant to their work. The focus of the process may be a certain technique or framework, but it could also be the development of new curriculum, the use of new materials, or any other aspect of teaching that requires improvement. In peer coaching, the participants decide what to focus on in light of their current needs and levels of expertise.

It is up to the individuals being coached to decide on the type of coaching they need: mirror coaching, collaborative coaching, or expert coaching. Each promotes a different level of reflection and awareness. In order for practitioners to make this decision freely, they should be reassured that such information will not be disclosed to others. Confidentiality is a particularly important characteristic of peer coaching, and helps to promote what Noddings (1984) calls an "ethic of caring"—a perspective that enhances trust and self-esteem and allows participants to focus on the task at hand while withholding unnecessary judgment.

Because the cycles of peer coaching—needs assessment, preparation for observation, observation, and reflection—can repeat indefinitely, they can best be visualized as components of a spiral (Figure 5.2).

5.2 Spiral Diagram of Peer Coaching

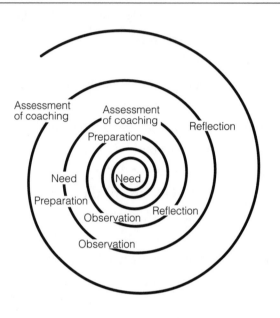

Classroom Observation

Classroom observation is an integral component of coaching. All educators have experienced these at one time or another, and can easily recall the nervousness such visits engender. By establishing confidentiality and prearranging what the focus of the observation will be, coaching partners can dramatically diminish anxiety. Usually, observations focus on specific teacher or student behaviors, such as the following:

- Delivery of instructions
- Classroom management
- Student engagement
- Use of a second language (foreign-language and ESL courses)

- Patterns of interaction
- Clarity of explanations

The observer's task consists of recording the presence or absence of these behaviors in class. Though schools often have standardized observation protocols, behaviors selected on the basis of the coached teacher's needs are, naturally, best. Coaches can distinguish their colleague's needs by reflecting on their stage of professional development. For example, if a coached teacher is at Stage 3 of Fletcher's mentoring model (see Chapter 3), the coach should focus on specific behaviors that constrain the coached teacher's performance, and only later in the process switch gears to explore the effect of specific actions on students. It would be harmful for a coach to require that a coached teacher know exactly how to respond to the specific needs of all learners when that teacher is still grappling with basic classroom management issues. This is not to say that coaches have to refrain from encouraging their colleagues forward; simply that coaches not mechanically follow "tick or cross" observation procedures that disregard the developmental nature of the coaching relationship.

One classroom observation process that has received particular attention in recent years, mainly because of its developmental focus, is Charlotte Danielson in *Enhancing Professional Practice* (1996). Danielson suggests that there are four distinct domains to professional practice, each reflecting a set of fundamental teacher competencies (see Figure 5.3). Levels of performance for each competency range from novice to expert, allowing observations based on this framework to accommodate teachers' distinct developmental rhythms.

Danielson's framework is appealing because it approaches teacher growth as a nonlinear process that involves some regression in addition to overall progress. If introduced at the beginning of the coaching

5.3 Charlotte Danielson's Framework for Professional Practice

Domain 1: Planning and Preparation
- Knowledge of contents and pedagogy
- Knowledge of learners
- Learning goals
- Knowledge of resources
- Instructional design
- Assessment

Domain 2: The Classroom Environment
- Creating an environment of respect and rapport
- Establishing a culture for learning
- Managing classroom procedures
- Managing learner behavior
- Organizing physical space

Domain 3: Instruction
- Communicating clearly and accurately
- Using questioning and discussion techniques
- Engaging learners in learning
- Feedback to learners
- Flexibility and responsiveness

Domain 4: Professional Responsibilities
- Reflecting on teaching
- Maintaining accurate records
- Communicating with families
- Contributing to the school
- Growing and developing professionally
- Showing professionalism

Source: Adapted from Danielson (1996).

process, the framework can help coaches and colleagues reflect on the context of the actions being observed, while also suggesting where future observations and other development strategies should be targeted.

Maximizing Observation

Many researchers agree that observation can be best carried out in three stages (Cogan, 1973; Costa and Garmston, 2002; Fletcher, 2000; Garman, 1982; Glanz, 2000; Goldhammer, 1969; Goldsberry, 1986; Marczely, 2001). In the first stage, coaches and colleagues confer prior to the actual observation. This conference fulfills different purposes, such as disclosing the teacher's intentions, helping the teacher reflect on her intentions and make changes to the original plan, and allowing the teacher to mentally rehearse the class in order to gain a fuller awareness of what to expect. Following the pre-observation conference—which Costa and Garmston (2002) refer to as the "Planning Conversation"—the actual observation can take place. To be carried out effectively, both coach and coached teacher should play active roles in providing focus and direction. In the third stage, the coaching pair reflects on the classroom observation.

This approach is generally referred to as clinical supervision (Cogan, 1973; Garman, 1982; Goldhammer, 1969; Marczely, 2001). Though it has been criticized for reducing observation to a series of prescribed steps and fostering an imbalance of power—with the teacher being disempowered and the coach setting the agenda—this is still the most common type of supervision, largely because of its focus on teacher improvement.

Barone (1998) contrasts the triune model of clinical supervision with an alternative "artistic approach" to observation:

In an artistic approach there are two basic phases of the supervisory process. These two phases correspond to two fundamental activities of the supervisor as he or she attempts to achieve the primary goal of supervision. . . . The first is the phase of appreciation. In this part of the process, the supervisor observes, interprets, and makes judgments about the qualities within the educational events at hand. . . . The second phase is that of disclosure in which the supervisor publicizes the elements of artistry that he or she has come to appreciate, and invites reactions to and discussion about the content of the observations disclosed. (p. 1105; see also Eisner, 1982)

Costa and Garmston (2002) suggest yet another method of observation—cognitive coaching—which I believe is the approach most helpful to teachers. While not departing from the three-stage model of clinical supervision, cognitive coaching structures each stage as a road map for coach-colleague interaction. As the authors note, "A map can be thought of as an internal representation, or a scaffold, that displays the territory in a goal-oriented conversation. Knowing the territory, in this sense, allows the coach to make a conscious choice from the various routes that may be taken" (p. 53).

According to Costa and Garmston, the coach should serve as a mediator, helping the coached teacher "to analyze a problem and develop her own problem-solving strategies" and "set up strategies for self-monitoring during the problem-solving process" (2002, p. 58). This conceptualization empowers the coach to encourage proactive engagement on the part of the coached teacher, and is in line with the principles of adult learning discussed in Chapter 1.

Preparation

The first thing prospective coaches and coached teachers need to do is lay the groundwork for their work together. The coach may visit the coached teacher's class to get a feel for her teaching, join with the coached teacher to analyze a video of classroom instruction, or use a framework such as Danielson's to reflect on areas for improvement. As noted in Chapter 2, the first stage in a collaborative process is usually characterized both by high motivation and by overreliance on leaders. In Chapter 3, we saw how overdependence on mentors can cause colleagues to emulate their mentors at the expense of their own development. This is particularly likely during coaching because of the more intimate nature of the relationship. To avoid such pitfalls, coaches should remember that their main duty is to further their colleagues' agendas.

Preparation helps teachers clarify goals, specify success indicators, and establish personal learning foci and processes for assessing the lesson observed. During this stage, the coach should probe the coached teacher's educational philosophy to determine focal points for the observation (see Figure 5.4). The coach should encourage the coached teacher to articulate the main goals of the observation, and the coached teacher should tell the coach what to look for during the lesson. Together the two colleagues should devise a way to verify whether or not the coached teacher's goals have been achieved.

The preparation stage allows the coached teacher a chance to walk through the lesson plan beforehand—a process that can help the teacher perform better later on without external direction. During this stage, the teacher can assess the effectiveness of the proposed lesson with the aid of a colleague, as a way both of disclosing intentions

5.4 Suggested Observational Foci

A survey of over 50 teachers suggested the following areas as good focal points for observation.	
Domain	**Suggested Foci**
Teacher	• Clarity of language • Knowledge of subject • Gestures and other mannerisms • Instructions • Management of group activities • Use of resources • Pacing • Use of time
Students	• On-task vs. off-task behaviors • Interactions (teacher to student, student to student, students to students, student to teacher) • Attention levels • Adherence to instructions • Difficulties with the material • Recordkeeping of teacher's work • Facility with testing methods
Classroom activities	• Adequacy with regard to student skill levels • Adequacy with regard to lesson goals • Level of differentiation provided • Variety of activities • Sequencing of activities • Transitions between activities
Classroom environment	• Classroom setup • Teacher talk vs. student talk • Classroom decorations and their use • Strategies for grouping students • Use of classroom resources (e.g., chalkboard)

and spotting potential pitfalls. Engaging in this reflective skill lays the groundwork for future independent reflection on the teacher's part.

The coached teacher should verbally describe every step of her upcoming lesson to the coach. The power of this exercise cannot be overstated: it allows the coached teacher to track the evolution of her lesson plan aloud—thus allowing her to determine precise focal points for the observation and shifting her perspective to that of observer. The coach's task is to challenge the teacher to provide reasons for her actions during the lesson. The following three kinds of questions can help:

1. **Framing Questions.** Expand the discussion of the lesson to include new ideas, helping to establish relationships among issues.
2. **Exploratory Questions.** Clarify, expand on, or provide a reason for information presented in the lesson.
3. **Sensing Questions.** Coax emotional responses to determine affective issues that may affect the lesson.

See Figure 5.5 for a rundown of the steps necessary to successfully prepare for an observation.

Methods of Observation

Different observational focal points require different recording methods. Figures 5.6–5.9 show examples of techniques for tracking classroom events during observation. Figure 5.6 shows a coach's recording of classroom interactions. It's clear from the image that the teacher being observed used a lockstep approach—dominating the action and arranging the students in neat rows—that is not conducive to student interaction. Students at the back are not integrated to the class; some of them are interacting, but not with the lesson.

For the observation represented in Figure 5.7, the coached teacher had asked the coach to observe her students' levels of engagement with four activities she'd planned for the day. The chart suggests that Activity C was particularly hard for students to follow—only four students managed to complete the activity while the rest did not even attempt it, choosing instead to remain off-task.

5.5 Preparing for Observation

Step 1. Clarifying Goals
Answer the following questions:
- Is observation the most effective way to tackle the issue at hand?
- How long should the observation be?
- What specific aspects of the mentee's teaching will the coach observe?

Step 2. Specifying Evidence
Answer the following questions:
- What evidence should the coach gather during the observation?
- How frequently should the coach gather evidence?
- How much evidence should the coach gather?
- How will the coach gather evidence?

Step 3. Establishing a Personal Development Focus
Answer the following questions:
- What does the coach want to learn from the observation?
- What does the mentee expect to learn from the observation?

Step 4. Previewing the Lesson
The mentee verbally previews the upcoming class for the coach. This narrative may lead the mentee to reconsider or amend her original plan.

Step 5. Determining Self-Assessment Procedures
Answer the following questions:
- How will the mentee know whether or not objectives have been achieved?
- How will the coach know that data gathered from the observation is valid and reliable?

Step 6. Assessing the Effectiveness of Preparation
Answer the following questions:
- How useful has this preparation been?
- What problems have the participants encountered?
- What caused these problems?
- How can these problems be overcome in future sessions?

5.6 Sample Record of Classroom Interaction

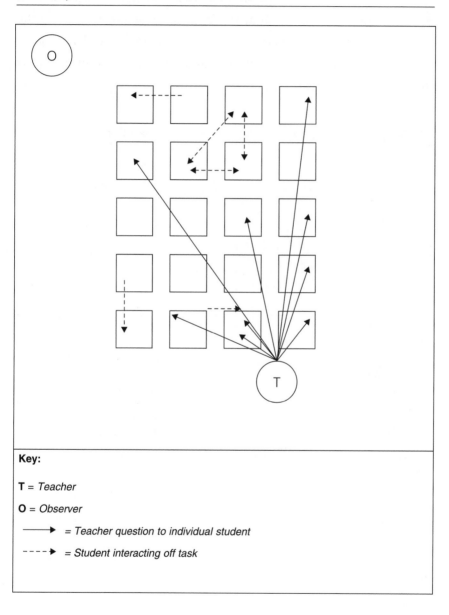

Key:

T = *Teacher*

O = *Observer*

⟶ = *Teacher question to individual student*

---▶ = *Student interacting off task*

Figure 5.8 shows how a coach recorded a teacher's movement in the classroom. The coach sat at the front of the classroom during the observation and used stars on her chart, numbered in order, to show the teacher's position at six-minute intervals. The illustration shows that the teacher began and concluded his lesson by standing at the

5.7 Sample Record of On-Task vs. Off-Task Student Behavior

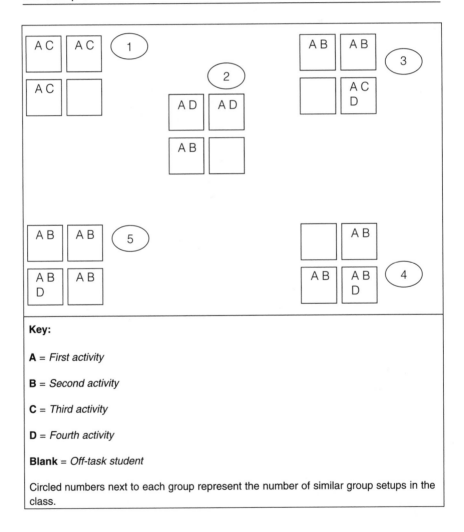

Key:

A = *First activity*

B = *Second activity*

C = *Third activity*

D = *Fourth activity*

Blank = *Off-task student*

Circled numbers next to each group represent the number of similar group setups in the class.

5.8 Sample Record of Teacher Movement

The teacher in this scenario asked the coach to record his movement in the classroom. The coach decided to sit at the front of the room, and indicated each position the teacher moved to by placing a star wherever the teacher was standing every six minutes. The stars are numbered chronologically.

As we can see, the teacher began and finished the lesson by standing at the front of the room. There are recurring patterns of movement, where the teacher moves close to certain students; we might speculate that these students either misbehaved or frequently requested the teacher's presence. Overall, the diagram suggests that the teacher has trouble following a logical sequence when providing feedback to students.

front. The figure also shows that the teacher moved repeatedly in the direction of certain students; during reflection, the coach and coached teacher might surmise that these students either called for the teacher or otherwise caught his attention.

Unlike the other sample recordings, Figure 5.9 is all text. The coached teacher in this case wanted to improve her feedback skills, so she asked the coach to note and time her interaction with the class. The coach responded by recording in a ledger-style chart every discrete action taken by the teacher and students.

Reflection

Following the observation, the coach and coached teacher should get together to reflect on the data gathered. As Costa and Garmston (2002) note, reflection helps teachers "to maximize the construction of significant meanings from the experience and to apply those insights to other settings and events" (p. 41). John Heron (1990) suggests that there are two basic types of reflection—authoritative and facilitative—with three subcategories each. His model of intervention helps outline the coach's role in fostering this reflection.

Authoritative

- **Prescriptive.** The coach tells the coached teacher what to do.
- **Informative.** The coach provides the coached teacher with new knowledge.
- **Confronting.** The coach tries to raise the coached teacher's consciousness by challenging her on problematic areas that she may not have noticed.

5.9 Sample Record of Time Use and Sequencing

Teacher: Margaret	Date: September 28	Grade: 3rd
Teacher	**Students**	**Minutes Elapsed**
1. Teacher greets class and explains my presence	Students greet teacher and me	2
2. Teacher hands out corrected tests	Students look at their tests and talk to each other	5
3. Teacher reads Exercise 1 (reading comprehension) and asks students for correct answers	Some students volunteer answers. Disorder. Should ask them to put their hands up	3
4. Teacher reads Exercise 2 (finding synonyms in the text) and asks students for correct answers	Five students provide correct answers. The rest?	7
5. Teacher reads Exercise 3 (fill-in-the-blanks with the correct form of the verb) and asks students for correct answers	Two students volunteer answers. The rest?	4
6. Teacher goes to board and draws a table to explain the present perfect tense	Students copy table in notebooks	8
7. Teacher drills sample sentences from table	Students repeat sentences	2
8. Teacher asks students to work in pairs and do Exercise 3 again	Pairs redo exercise	12
9. Teacher asks for correct answers	Same two students and three others volunteer correct answers	2
10. Teacher explains the present perfect again and provides the right answers to Exercise 3	Students copy chart again!!! Why? Then copy answers teacher dictates	7
11. Teacher asks four students to read the composition sections of their tests	Students read. Rest of class oblivious (look at watch, chat, pack their materials, etc.)	8
12. Bell rings. Teacher dismisses class	Students rush out of class before being dismissed	—

Facilitative

- **Cathartic.** The coach draws feelings and emotions from the coached teacher.
- **Catalytic.** The coach encourages the coached teacher's self-discovery by questioning her on critical areas, so that she can let off steam. Whereas the authoritative coach explicitly prescribes the areas to focus on in the confronting phase, the facilitative coach encourages the teacher to determine these areas herself by discussing her feelings about the lesson.
- **Supportive.** The coach affirms the coached teacher's worth by praising her achievements.

Heron warns that if the session revolves around the coach's rather than the coached teacher's agenda, authoritative reflection can become authoritarian, and facilitative reflection abdicating.

The Teacher's Choice Framework distinguishes among three types of reflection sessions, during which coaches may use any of Heron's interventions:

1. **Mirroring Coaching.** The coach gives the observation data to the coached teacher, who analyzes them away from the coach.
2. **Expert Coaching.** The coach analyzes the observation data and offers suggestions.
3. **Collaborative Coaching.** The coach gives the observation data to the coached teacher, and helps her to reflect on them. The coached teacher controls the agenda at all times, and the coach refrains from giving advice unless the coached teacher asks for it.

Because both the coach and the coached teacher need time to reflect on the observation before considering the data collected, they should devote the time immediately following the lesson to completing a post-observation reflection protocol (Figure 5.10).

5.10 Post-Observation Reflection Protocol

Coach: _____ Coached Teacher: _____ Date: _____ Class: _____ Time: _____ Focal points for this observation: _____		
What I Saw/Did	**What I Think About What I Saw/Did**	**What I Should Change About What I Saw/Did**

This form will provide the basis for the reflection session. In addition, teachers might consider structuring the session according to the following steps:

1. **Sharing Impressions.** The coach and coached teacher share their feelings about the class, noting areas of agreement.
2. **Reviewing Goals.** The coach and coached teacher assess the reliability of the data collected by the coach, and use the data to determine whether or not the original goals for the lesson were achieved.
3. **Assessing Cause and Effect.** The coach and coached teacher ponder the causes of actions discussed in the data.

4. **Exploring Alternatives.** If goals were not achieved during the lesson, the coach and coached teacher explore possible changes to the lesson plan.

5. **Summarizing the Process.** The coach and coached teacher each summarize what they learned from the coaching process, assess its effectiveness, and set goals for further coaching.

– 6 –

Professional Development Through Writing

Writing, like life itself, is a voyage of discovery.

—Henry Miller

Josh

Josh has taught science for the past fifteen years, and has collaborated in numerous professional development initiatives, from colleague-to-colleague coaching to the usual in-service workshops. Teaching at a typical urban school, he is always looking for signs of student failure and works hard to help his students succeed.

At an education conference last year, Josh attended a workshop on the power of writing as a reflective tool for teachers. This encouraged him to start tracking his students' progress through field notes. He began jotting down observations about notable classroom events, which he would later reflect upon when preparing lessons or units.

These notes helped Josh discern patterns in his interaction with students.

Soon, Josh found himself reviewing professional books and journal articles about writing as a learning tool, creating new learning tasks for his classes, and sharing his insights with colleagues. He also prepared a portfolio to help him communicate his and his students' progress to others in the school. He started it by laying out his educational philosophy—the unifying set of principles that guided his teaching. He set a clear goal for the portfolio, divided it into sections, and asked other science teachers in the school to comment on his reflections and on the events he wrote about. With this input, he developed a reflective statement about his development process that summarized his findings for the rest of the faculty.

In addition to his portfolio Josh kept a journal that he shared with two other science teachers on a weekly basis. This collaborative reflection lasted for about six months and provided relevant insights into the transformations taking place in Josh's classroom.

The school principal supported Josh's reflective writing process by allowing him and his two journal partners time to meet, and by asking him to share his portfolio with other teachers during in-service days. These presentations were so successful that Josh was asked to repeat them at a local conference; he was also asked to coach new science teachers at the school, and to submit an article to a peer-reviewed journal.

Josh used three writing tools to deepen his understanding of teaching and learning in the classroom: field notes, portfolios, and dialogue journals. In his case, the three tools merged into one another and became mutually supportive. However, other teachers may choose to use only one of the tools, or to use them in conjunction with other professional development strategies. The use of writing as a support for reflection, and the systematic collection of evidence about teaching and learning, are powerful tools for those who choose to pursue their professional development individually. Teachers who engage in self-directed professional development still need to reinforce their bonds with others. Josh started his exploration on an individual basis, but progressively extended his reflection process to include other colleagues and the wider school community; by sharing his writing with peers, he helped contribute to their professional development as well.

Field Notes

As shown in Figure 6.1, there are seven distinct steps to keeping field notes (Brison & Leavitt, 1999). Teachers begin by writing down a running description of an event, either in their planning notebooks or in specifically constructed field notebooks (see Figure 6.2). Lofland (1995) suggests that notes should be devoid of inference, summary, or abstraction, and serve simply as a "raw" description of an experience. Appropriate experiences for note-taking include overheard comments, observations about students, and conversations among and with students.

According to Umphrey (2001), notes help teachers improve recall by making them concentrate on things they might not otherwise notice. He elaborates:

> Documenting experiences of both inner and outer worlds is a basic step of all the arts and sciences, the raw material of human progress. Converting experience to symbolic representation is the basis of all the disciplines. Though one reason for making field notes is to

6.1 Guidelines for Developing Field Notes

1. Devote regular time to working on your notes. Be systematic about collecting the notes during class and reflecting on them as soon after class has finished as you can. This way, you will be able to recall the event as faithfully as possible.

2. Start by expanding your "raw" notes into full sentences or paragraphs. Remember to remain objective about the event. During this stage you only want to recall the events as they happened. Refrain from interpreting or summarizing the event.

3. Analyze your feelings. How did you feel as a consequence of the particular event? How did students feel? Was there any indication of feelings in the students' behavior? How do you know?

4. Try to explain the event and jot down preliminary ideas, generalizations, and conclusions that you derive from the experience.

5. As you develop the different sections of your field notes, write down questions you still have.

6. Think of resources and actions that can help you disclose answers to your questions. Make a schedule for accessing those resources.

7. Write down your final conclusions.

prepare you to create more finished products later, the notes themselves can become important historical documents.

Reflection occurs when teachers expand on their notes by trying to explain the events observed. This process need not occur in one day—many teachers carry out sustained observations on events in order to discern patterns of behavior over time. Either way, teachers may consult with colleagues, carry out bibliographic research, ask peers to sit in on lessons, and test new ideas in the classroom to aid their reflection. Whether conclusions remain temporary or evolve into personal living theories, their effects will be enhanced by collaboration.

6.2 Sample Field Notebook Page

Date:_____ Time:_____ Class:_____ Summary of the event:				
The Event	**Explanations and Elaborations**	**How You Feel About the Event**	**What You Think About the Event**	**Lingering Questions**
Conclusions				

Dialogue Journals

Dialogue journals (Figure 6.3) are conversations in writing. Teachers may choose to keep dialogue journals when they cannot meet with colleagues in person but wish to assist in each other's development by writing and responding to one another. Journal entries usually consist of either reactions to or reflections on events, people, or ideas related to practice. Reactive entries are cathartic, consisting of the teachers' feelings; reflective entries are evaluative, consisting of assessments or observations. Both types should be subjective, conveying the teachers' opinions or predictions; as such, they provide a safe haven for highly critical discourse between peers.

6.3 Sample Dialogue Journal Pages

| Date: _____ Writer: _____ |
| Reader: _____ Topic: _____ |

Writer's Comments	Reader's Comments

Dialogue journals are used extensively in Language Arts and ESL courses as a way to foster language and literacy development. In the context of professional development, they are powerful professional learning tools based on the idea that writing promotes learning by allowing teachers to explore areas of personal and professional interest together. Journal entries give teachers the power to wonder aloud and connect in writing with the opinions of colleagues, thus clarifying and reflecting on their own perceptions (Sweeney, 1995).

Dialogue journals are much more personal than field notes. Journal writing allows professionals to distance themselves from events, giving them time to reflect on their situation. As Roderick (1986) notes, dialogue journals allow teachers to become "co-participants, co-creators . . . and co-constructors of the educational experience" (p. 308).

The feedback on classroom dilemmas that colleagues provide in their journal entries tends to be more open and focused than that provided in the context of other development strategies. However, it is very important for teachers to have a high interest in the topic at hand, as well as high levels of mutual trust and respect, for the feedback to be worthwhile.

Dialogue journals also help teachers take a more scholastic approach to their profession. Allchin (1998) highlights the important relationship between scholarship and collaborative research:

> Scholars are familiar with the professional dimensions of research, including the sharing of research with peers, especially for evaluation. . . . Rehearsing the generally familiar aspects of peer review in research is valuable in eliciting parallel thoughts about teaching. . . . In a broad view, scholarship is worthless if not shared.

Lacking the explicatory benefit of inflection or body language, journal-entry discussions are naturally more ambiguous than spoken conversations. Teachers should therefore take care to word their entries in plain and constructive language. Brinton, Holter, and Goodwin (1993) suggest the following guidelines for responding to journal entries:

- Respond directly and personally.
- Be sensitive to your peer's experience. Dialogue journals perform an affective function and thus require a positive tone.
- Direct the writer's attention to patterns that you, as a reader, can perceive.
- Share your own experiences or those of other peers as a way of scaffolding reflection by providing alternative points of view.
- Be honest. Express honest opinions and avoid false confidence building.
- Ask questions, prompt more reflection.

In devising reflective entries, teachers might consider Darling-Hammond's (1998) categories of teacher knowledge:

- Subject matter
- How ideas connect across fields
- Student understanding
- Student beliefs
- Child and adolescent development
- How to communicate more sensitively with students and peers
- Student differences

A list of these categories can serve as a point of departure for journal explorations, or in seeking to explain classroom events. Journal partners may add additional categories to the list as their work evolves.

Portfolios

Professional portfolios have been used systematically by educators over the past twenty years to provide evidence of professional growth; because they are process-oriented, they help teachers remain continuously aware of their development. As Wilcox and Tomei (1999) put it:

> Creating portfolios requires systemic self-assessment and allows teachers to experience the power of their own reflective thinking— thinking which can, and often does, result in new and better ways of teaching. Research shows that responding to reading in writing, sharing ideas, and reflecting on the various "ways of knowing" are processes that indeed enhance learning and improve thinking. Practicing reflective thinking strategies, as easy as "thinking about your thinking process," enables a good thinker to become a better thinker. (p. 11)

Knapper and Wright (2001) note the many possible nonevaluative uses of portfolios:

> In addition to their use for tenure, promotion, and annual performance reviews, portfolios have been employed in the preparation of teaching award files, as a post facto means of articulating an approach to teaching by award winners, as an exemplary document by senior faculty, as a "legacy" document by retiring departmental "builders" or pioneers, as developmental files by graduate teaching assistants, as a part of documentation submitted for a job search, and as a source of evidence for the accreditation of teaching competence. (p. 25)

Bullock and Hawk (2001) define a portfolio as "an organized, goal-driven collection of documents . . . a collection that tells a story" (p. 8). They describe a portfolio as having four basic components:

1. **A specific purpose.** Though they are most frequently used for evaluating teacher progress, or as criteria for teacher certification, portfolios are most useful for professional development purposes.

2. **A specific audience.** If a portfolio is used for professional development, the audience will usually be the teacher herself.

3. **Work samples, or "evidence."** The teachers themselves decide what constitutes adequate evidence and are responsible for gathering and reflecting on it. As Knapper and Wright (2001) explain:

    [A] key principle of the teaching portfolio is that the content, organization, and presentation are controlled by the individual teacher. There have been attempts in the past to "automate" portfolios by providing fill-in-the-box computerized forms, but this undermines the underlying philosophy of the portfolio approach, which has the advantage of allowing different teachers to tailor a portfolio to their own needs. (p. 22)

4. **Teacher reflection.** Because portfolios require teachers to actively and continuously reflect on the evidence they collect, reflection is at once the main component and the principal outcome of portfolios.

According to Bullock and Hawk (2001), there are three main types of portfolios:

1. **Process portfolios** are intended to assess teacher progress in one or more areas over a given period of time.
2. **Product portfolios** may be part of a process portfolio; they concentrate on documenting progress towards a single specific area.
3. **Showcase portfolios** serve as collections of a teacher's best work.

In process and product portfolios, it is important that teachers display both successes and failures in order to accurately chronicle development, and that the amount of evidence presented suit the portfolio's purpose. Though these types of portfolios generally incorporate between five and ten pieces of evidence, teachers may choose to document their development further. A good strategy is to share the portfolio with critical friends before assembling the final version, in order to gauge whether the amount of evidence is sufficient.

Portfolios can be used at all levels of the Teacher's Choice Framework. For example, showcase portfolios are ideal for Level 1 teachers, who need to account for their level of expertise; process portfolios are suited to Level 3 teachers, who need to become progressively aware of their own improvements; and product portfolios, which are more finely focused, are especially helpful to Level 4 teachers searching for greater knowledge and awareness.

Portfolios should start by laying out the teacher's educational philosophy or platform, and should be divided into sections with corresponding entries and evidence. For instance, a teacher who wishes to implement a new curriculum model may choose to structure his portfolio into a planning section, a teaching section, and an assessment section. The planning section might include samples of curriculum or unit plans, original activities designed by the teacher, or summaries or critiques of relevant literature; the teaching section may contain photos, diagrams, videos, or even written transcripts of lessons; and the assessment section may present samples of tests or student portfolios. The evidence should be accompanied by captions that explain the reasons behind their inclusion in the portfolio and the ways in which they substantiate the teacher's development.

Figure 6.4 shows different types of possible portfolio evidence.

Bullock and Hawk (2001) suggest that there are three components to thorough reflection, which teachers should consider when writing portfolio entry captions:

1. **Description.** Teachers clearly indicate the who, what, where, why, and how of the entries.
2. **Analysis.** Teachers break the evidence down into parts and highlight surprising or puzzling issues, agreements, and disagreements between their prior knowledge and the issue raised by the evidence, as well as the strengths and weaknesses of the evidence in light of the portfolio goals.
3. **Planning.** Teachers "write about how the evidence has affected them and what implications it has for their future actions" (Bullock & Hawk, 2001, p. 16).

Most researchers agree that portfolios should include a table of contents, such as the sample in Figure 6.5.

6.4 Sample Portfolio Evidence

Possible Portfolio Section	Possible Evidence
Teaching	• Teacher-created activities, materials, assessments, and curriculum units • Lesson and unit plans • Individualized plans • Teacher observation protocols • Videos and photographs of teaching in action
Reflection	• Summary of teacher's personal educational philosophy • Field notes • Position papers • Personal and dialogue journals • Teacher's class management platform
Professional Development	• Teacher's professional development plan • Sample development activities • Summaries and critiques of professional literature • Relevant publications • Papers presented by teacher • Samples of projects in which the teacher participated • Research briefs • Proof of membership to professional organizations
Assessment	• Student assessments of teacher, materials, or activities • Teacher self-assessments • Administrator and peer assessment of teacher • Assessment of students • Student grades • Student portfolio samples • School or district subject standards
Resources	• List of relevant Web sites • Annotated reading lists • Quotes from education leaders • Diagrams, sketches, and photographs • Videos
School Community	• Teacher correspondence with students, parents, and colleagues • Proof of teacher collaborations in and contributions to the school community • Meeting minutes

6.5 Josh's Table of Contents

---

1. My goal

2. My beliefs about teaching and learning science

3. Before the professional development process:
   a. Reading log on Understanding by Design
   b. Initial UbD unit
   c. Students' comments
   d. Field notes on teaching the initial unit
   e. Photos of student work

4. During the professional development process:
   a. Dialogue journal with Kathy on implementing UbD
   b. Colleague observation protocol that Kathy and I developed
   c. Video of the observed class
   d. Kathy's comments
   e. Students' comments on the lesson
   f. Pre- and post-assessment of students

5. After the professional development process:
   a. Dialogue journal with Kathy and Peter
   b. Article on UbD
   c. Transparencies for presentation on science unit

6. Final reflections

Education Platforms

All acts of teaching are value-laden, so it is important for teachers to make their values known. Before creating a portfolio, teachers should put their teaching philosophy in writing. This is not a list of intentions or idealizations, but a concrete explanation of the reasons behind a teacher's actions. As such, it may make reference to teacher-student relations, expected outcomes of a particular course, how the learning environment is structured, teacher attitudes and motivations, and conceptions about teaching and learning.

Sergiovanni and Starratt (2002) suggest that all educational platforms should include teacher's views on the following:

- The aim of education
- Knowledge
- The social significance of student learning
- The teacher's concept of what it means to be a learner, what the curriculum is about, and the roles of teachers in mediating the encounter between students and curriculum
- Their preferred forms of pedagogy and school climate

As Allchin (1998) explains, a teaching philosophy is:

> [A] phrase used by different authors, [with] a wide variety of meanings. Many writers use it to refer to one's notions about how teaching occurs. We prefer to call such concepts "theories of learning." Presumably, such theories can be tested and supported by (or found contradictory to) evidence. Although they may be part of someone's personal beliefs, they are ultimately a matter for public consensus based on empirical study.

Writing about your professional values—that is, making your educational philosophy explicit—is not always easy, so Haugen (1998) suggests that teachers ask themselves the following questions as a warm-up:

- To what end am I teaching?
- By what means?
- To what degree?
- Why?

Alternatively, teachers can use Freire's (1996) self-directing questions:
- For whom,
- For what,

- Against whom, and
- Against what will this specific action work?

Reflective Summaries

All teachers should include summaries at the end of their portfolios that explain how the different evidence and reflections reflect their educational platforms. This final statement should aim to interpret the portfolio data and substantiate its validity.

Reflective summaries may do any of the following:

- Reveal the connections between different evidence
- Highlight significant trends that emerge from the evidence
- Further articulate the educational platform through examples
- Expand on the meaning of certain evidences
- Discuss any portfolio-related changes to the teacher's educational philosophy
- Suggest possible ways to further refine the teacher's practice
- Assess how much the portfolio development process has contributed to the teacher's development

When assessing the portfolio's effectiveness, teachers may want to invite colleagues to provide their perspectives. A good forum for this is a "portfolio exhibit conference," where teachers who have developed portfolios get together to comment on one another's evidence and reflections using individually or collaboratively designed rubrics (see Figure 6.6).

6.6 Sample Portfolio Appraisal Rubric

Circle whatever bullet points you agree with. The category with the most circled bullet points reflects the level of competence the portfolio displays.

1. The portfolio reflects superior competence.

- Presentation is thorough, well-organized, and informative
- Evidence shows clear progress towards portfolio goals
- Evidence clearly shows the effects of teaching on learning
- Reflections are thoughtful and related to future goals

2. The portfolio reflects competence.

- Presentation is well-organized and informative
- Evidence shows progress toward portfolio goals
- Evidence partially captures the effects of teaching on learning
- Reflections discuss patterns related to future goals

3. The portfolio reflects minimal competence.

- Captions for some pieces of evidence are informed
- Connection between goals and evidence is unclear
- Evidence concentrates mostly on teaching and very little on learning
- Reflections do not connect patterns to future goals

4. The portfolio reflects incompetence.

- Presentation is poor, with few entries and little information
- Connection between goals and evidence is left undisclosed
- Evidence does not refer to students' learning and is not effectively organized
- Reflections do not discuss patterns

Writing and the Teacher's Choice Framework

Though writing-focused strategies are particularly suited to individual work, their benefits are enhanced when teachers collaborate with colleagues and use them in conjunction with other development strategies. Because field notes help make teachers more aware of their actions in the classroom, they are particularly well suited for those at Level 1 or 2 of the Teacher's Choice Framework: those at Level 1 can use them to disclose their own living theories about teaching and learning, whereas those at Level 2 can use them to gain greater awareness of their competence levels. Dialogue journals, which promote collegial reflection, are best suited to teachers at Levels 2 and 3, who need both greater awareness and more knowledge; portfolios, which can be used to track progress at any level, are suitable for teachers at all levels of the framework.

– 7 –

Critical Development Teams

Human activity consists of action and reflection; it is praxis; it is transformation of the world. And as praxis, it requires theory to illuminate it. Human activity is theory and practice; it is reflection and action.

—Paulo Freire (1970, p. 125)

Jack's Story

Lincoln Bilingual School is a private K–6 school in South America. Students attend school for eight hours a day, and are taught a government-mandated core curriculum. Lessons are conducted in Spanish in the morning and English in the afternoon. Until four years ago, classes taught in English revolved around an ESL textbook and corresponding workbook, which did not incorporate subject matter content and merely drilled students in English grammar. Though the textbook helped students practice their listening and speaking skills, the students still had trouble communicating fluently and had difficulty understanding oral texts. The school's Board of Directors hired Jack, an ESL expert, to help.

Jack's first course of action was to work with the English teachers to revise the curriculum. He encouraged interdisciplinary work, and had English teachers teach part of the curriculum in English. After four intensive weeks of in-service workshops on how to teach language through content, the English teachers put their new skills to the test in the classroom. It wasn't long before they ran into difficulty. By conducting classroom observations, the teachers came to realize that they had substituted the ESL textbook for the subject matter content, and were selecting lessons on the basis of the grammar issues they raised. In other words, their teaching was still focused on grammar rather than communication. Content-based instruction requires teachers to use relevant subject matter content as the vehicle for language acquisition.

Jack decided the English teachers needed more help adapting to their new roles. K–3 and 4–6 teachers were free for one hour on Tuesdays and Thursdays, respectively, so Jack started holding staff meetings at those times, during which teachers could contribute lesson or unit plans that they felt had successfully relayed content to students. The meetings were structured so that teachers took turns acting as facilitators and devising agendas for interaction.

At each meeting, a teacher had ten minutes to present her plan to the others, who were expected to refrain from speaking while she did so. Following the presentation, the group had ten minutes to ask the presenter questions, which the presenter had another ten minutes to answer. A five-minute break ensued, during which the presenter convened with Jack while the other teachers discussed the plan. Following the break, the presenter worked with the other teachers to draw up conclusions. The final 15 minutes of the meeting were spent extrapolating best practices from the presentation. All interactions were recorded, and a designated secretary kept minutes of the meetings.

During the first year, the focus of these meetings was on implementing content-based instruction. As time progressed, the teachers started discussing other issues too, including classroom management, technology use, and authentic assessment measures. Over the course of the next three years, the meetings evolved into a professional development activity, which helped teachers to better self-direct their classes and provided them with ample context-specific knowledge.

Today, the scheduling at Lincoln Bilingual School has changed to allow all teachers to participate in the meetings at the same time. Student performance has improved dramatically, and the teachers are working to publish the conclusions from their meetings.

Critical Development Teams

Critical development teams are small groups, usually of ten or fewer, that convene regularly to explore teaching and learning issues. Birchak and colleagues (1998) describe their involvement in such groups as follows:

> We saw the study group as a place where we could negotiate a shared agenda instead of having someone else's agenda imposed on us. We know that our focus was on recognizing collaborative dialogue as a way of thinking through our issues and concerns, rather than relying on outside experts. For us, the study group signaled that we were the experts and best communicators of our professional growth. (p. 13)

Sergiovanni and Starratt (2002) explain how a variation of critical development teams, known as lesson study, is carried out in Japan:

> In lesson study, groups of teachers meet regularly over a period of several times to design a new, or redesign an existing, lesson. This lesson is then implemented in view of colleagues who offer "critical friends'" feedback. This critique and the suggestions that accompany it are directed to the lesson itself rather than the teacher. Thus, if things do not go well, it is assumed that everyone must work harder to refine or perhaps redefine the lesson, not the person. (p. 252)

Boss (2000) explains the Japanese model by saying that:

> "*Kounaikenshuu*, a Japanese term that has no easy translation in the English language, describes a process that is foreign to most American schools: school-based professional development that Japanese teachers engage in throughout their careers. . . . The groups provide a context in which teachers are mentored and trained by their peers, and also a laboratory for the development and testing of new teaching techniques." (p. 4)

Small study groups can enhance performance by allowing teachers the chance to plan common or connected units, research innovative instructional strategies, and propose suggestions for improved practice. According to Murphy (1992), there should be no more than six members to a team, and groups should meet on a regular basis.

Defining Critical Development Teams

Critical development teams fulfill the following purposes:

- To reinforce, clarify, and deepen learning by providing the opportunity to reflect on common concerns.
- To provide feedback on team members' teaching and learning.
- To provide practical advice on ways to enhance student learning.
- To motivate teachers and make teaching more enjoyable.
- To help teachers grow professionally by allowing for collective educational leadership.

Because it is easy for teams to deviate from their original purposes, we should also bear in mind that critical development teams are *not*

- Staff meetings where school policies are discussed.
- In-service training activities. Though teams may profit from the help of outside experts, their true value lies in the collective construction of answers to teacher questions.
- Cathartic. Teams should not spend time grieving about school problems, and should thrive on hope instead.

Critical development teams differ from other professional development activities in that they

- **Are voluntary.** This requirement comports with the tenet that teachers need to take charge of their own learning and development.

- **Challenge team member beliefs.** By collectively exploring alternatives to their current work methods, team members can construct context-specific instructional strategies based on their shared beliefs and values.
- **Integrate theory and practice.** Team members collaborate on different modes of reflection (see Chapter 4) to construct their own practical theories, which they in turn share with students, teachers, and administrators.
- **Contribute to building community.** Members create new identities for themselves within the school simply by volunteering to participate in teams. The proactive, collegial nature of teams promotes peer-to-peer support and enhances both the school climate and school culture.

Critical development teams can take many different forms, including the following (Birchak et al., 1998):

- **Job-alike groups.** Made up of teachers who hold the same position in different schools.
- **Topic-centered groups.** Made up of teachers from different schools who are interested in the same teaching or learning topic (e.g., implementation of new technologies in the classroom).
- **Teacher research groups.** Made up of teachers who want to share their personal inquiries.
- **Professional book discussion groups.** Made up of teachers who want to discuss a book or article they have all read.
- **Issues discussion groups.** Made up of teachers who share concerns about a professional development issue. Issues discussion groups differ from topic-centered groups in that the

teachers share a pressing need for development, rather than a more general common professional interest.

- **School-based groups.** Made up of teachers from the same school who want to discuss issues of mutual concern.

Developing Critical Development Teams

In their initial stages, critical development teams are characterized by high motivation but little or no direction. Despite their unifying purposes, teams can be hard to structure so that they are both focused and productive. To overcome this difficulty, teachers might consider introducing protocols. As Sergiovanni and Starratt (2002) note, "having some ground rules and using protocols to help guide the inquiry can help teachers be more comfortable with what is expected and how to participate in collegial activities. Protocols help assure teachers that the focus is on the study of teaching and not the evaluation of teachers" (p. 255). Blythe, Allen, and Schieffelin Powell (1999) suggest that protocols could revolve around the following issues:

- The quality of student work
- Instruction
- Student understanding
- Student growth
- Student intent

Any of these focal points can help teachers reflect on what it takes for their school to improve, as long as they are relevant to the team members' current practice. See Figure 7.1 for a form teams can use to determine which issues to focus on.

7.1 Nine Focusing Questions for Critical Development Teams

Answer the following questions individually and share the answers with your teammates.

1. How do your students learn? Why do they learn this way?
2. How do you teach? Why do you teach this way?
3. Is your teaching consistent with research on learning and teaching?
4. Is your teaching based on specific theories about learning and teaching? If so, which ones?
5. Are there alternative models of teaching that might better serve your students?
6. What learning experiences must your students have in order to succeed? How can you best provide these learning experiences?
7. What are some stumbling blocks in your teaching? Which of these do you want to explore?
8. How can your colleagues help you overcome your stumbling blocks?
9. How can your team best communicate its collective research?

All team protocols share certain steps in common. Most begin with an introductory phase, during which members agree on the purpose of their team. In the second phase, a presenter usually introduces an issue for discussion, which members mull over in the third phase. The presenter offers her perspective on the discussion in the fourth phase, and the entire team analyzes the discussion and draws up conclusions. The fifth and final phase is reserved for collaborative evaluation of the meeting. See Figure 7.2 for a sample Teacher's Choice Framework protocol.

Now contrast the protocol in Figure 7.2 with the one shown in Figure 7.3, which was devised for a Japanese Lesson Study model (Stigler & Hiebert, 1999), and with Seidel's (1998) protocol for a "collaborative assessment conference" in Figure 7.4. The protocol shown in Figure 7.2 is the most thorough, and thus the most useful for

7.2 Sample Protocol for a Critical Development Team

Phase	Purpose and Materials	Length in Minutes
1. Welcome and Housekeeping	The agenda for the meeting is read and accepted. Roles are distributed and materials are made available.	5 minutes
2. Presentation	Artifacts for study are presented. These can include journal articles, book chapters, videos, official documents, and samples of student or teacher work. Artifacts are selected prior to the meeting and presented by the selector while others listen silently.	10 minutes
3. First Impressions	Team members personally appraise the adequacy of the selected artifacts while the presenter silently writes down her impressions of her teammates' reactions.	10 minutes
4. Break	The presenter reviews her teammates' reactions and prepares her response to the team.	5 minutes
5. Initial Summary	The team chairperson summarizes the meeting so far and invites the presenter to respond to the team's comments.	5 minutes
6. Report	The presenter responds to the team's comments by referring to the presented artifacts while the team listens silently.	10 minutes
7. Probing	Team members ask the presenter questions using framing, exploratory, or sensing questions, with an aim toward reflection.	10 minutes
8. Final Summary and Implications	The chairperson asks the group to reflect on any lessons learned at the meeting. The secretary records any comments.	5 minutes
9. Adjourning	Participants assess the meeting and schedule the next one.	5 minutes

Source: Adapted from Díaz-Maggioli (in press).

7.3 Stigler and Hiebert's Japanese Lesson Study Steps

Step 1. Defining the problem
Step 2. Planning the lesson
Step 3. Teaching the lesson
Step 4. Evaluating the lesson and reflecting on its effect
Step 5. Revising the lesson
Step 6. Teaching the revised lesson
Step 7. Evaluating and reflecting again
Step 8. Sharing the results

Source: Adapted from Stigler and Hiebert (1999).

7.4 Seidel's Collaborative Assessment Conference Steps

- Getting started
- Describing the work
- Raising questions
- Speculating about what the teachers are working on
- Hearing from the presenter
- Discussing implications for teaching and learning
- Reflecting on the conference

Source: Adapted from Seidel (1998).

newly formed teams. The other two protocols may be used by more seasoned teams.

Teams that convene to discuss books or articles can also benefit from protocols. Figure 7.5 shows a sample protocol for such teams.

7.5 Professional Book Discussion Group Protocol

Step 1: Into (before the meeting). Team members agree on a book or collection of articles to read. Each team member is in charge of explicating a chapter or article to the
group using an activity-based presentation that connects the reading to the needs of the
school. Members set a presentation schedule. (There is generally one presentation per
meeting.)

Step 2: Through (during the meeting).

- Prior to each presentation, the chairperson briefly recaps the previous presentation
  or, in the case of inaugural meetings, clarifies the team's purpose. Participants can
  also use this time to share their reactions to the previous meeting (5 minutes).

- Team members present their chapter or articles, indicating clearly their relevance
  to the team's needs (30 minutes).

- During a break, team members reflect in writing on the sharing experience
  (5 minutes).

- Following the break, team members ask the presenters questions (5 minutes).

- Team members discuss the chapters or articles presented and their relevance to
  the school's needs (5 minutes).

- Team members volunteer conclusions, which are recorded in the minutes, and
  evaluate the session. The chairperson announces the topic of the next meeting
  and assigns a new reading (10 minutes).

Step 3: Beyond (after the meeting).

- Team members apply one of the key ideas from the meeting to their classroom
  practice, and collect evidence of their having done so to share with the group.

- Team members read the chapter or article for discussion at the next meeting.

Leading Team Meetings

If protocols help to structure meetings, roles provide direction and
help maximize meeting time (Doyle & Straus, 1982). Team members
should rotate roles so that everyone has a chance to be a leader. The
three key roles for critical development team management are as
follows:

- **Facilitator.** The facilitator is a neutral participant who helps the group focus its energies by organizing and mediating interactions during the meeting, protecting members from verbal attacks, and ensuring that everyone has a chance to participate actively. The facilitator's responsibilities include arranging the time and place for meetings, arriving early to set up the meeting space, providing all team members with the agenda and necessary materials, deciding whose turn it is to speak, keeping time, and helping the recorder record all relevant discussion points. During the meeting, the facilitator does not participate in the discussion, and instead focuses on making sure that the meeting progresses smoothly and the agenda is covered.
- **Recorder.** Like the facilitator, the recorder also refrains from the general discussion. This person serves as the team's memory, recording everything that is said in the discussion before prioritizing and synthesizing key points and forwarding them to all team members (usually within a week of the meeting). The recorder is also responsible for noting any conclusions or insights from each meeting in the team's minutes, which serve as a measure of team progress. Because he is not actively involved in the discussion, the recorder can objectively appraise members' contributions and sieve them for the benefit of the whole team.
- **Chairperson.** Unlike the facilitator and recorder, the chairperson does play an active role in each meeting— as a voice of authority. This individual works with the facilitator beforehand to develop a suitable agenda; during the meeting, she retains the power to alter the agenda if needed. Towards the end of each meeting, the chairperson makes

sure everyone is informed of what needs to be done prior to meeting again, assigning reading materials and key roles for next time.

Critical development teams are particularly suitable for teachers at Level 3 of the Teacher's Choice Framework, but can be greatly enhanced by including Level 1 teachers, who can help direct the discussions and activities.

– 8 –

Attending Conferences and Seminars

Tell me and I forget; teach me and I remember; involve me and I learn.
—Old Chinese proverb

Ruth's Story

Like other teachers in her district, Ruth has attended in-service day seminars and conferences since college. She finds these activities to be welcome breaks from the hard work in the classroom; she always gleans new ideas to apply to her classes, and they give her a sense of renewal. But there's also a downside. To start with, she finds that the one-shot nature of lectures and workshops leaves her little room to really explore the issues in depth. Ruth would welcome more follow-up activities, since it can be hard for teachers to implement new practices on their own. She also wishes she knew a better way to share her new knowledge with colleagues than by chatting in the staff lounge or presenting at staff meetings and in-service days.

128

When Ruth's district paid for her to participate in an international education conference last year, she took a more focused approach than usual. The four-day conference showcased the work of many respected teachers and researchers, and because she was the only person from her district to attend, she wanted to effectively communicate what she learned. She discovered a template for maximizing participation at big conferences in an article, based her schedule on it, and planned how to communicate her learning back to the district.

Before heading for the conference, Ruth researched the topics and presenters on the Web, set clear goals for each of the sessions, and organized her participation around a unifying theme. Once there, she attended presentations that were directly relevant to her professional concerns. Upon returning to school, she bound handouts and other resources from the conference into a package along with her own reflections on each of the sessions. She shared this package with her colleagues in the staff room, and also sent a copy to the district central office. The expertise Ruth gained by attending the conference led her to become involved in other professional development strategies, as well as to actively promote conference-going among her colleagues.

Realizing the Promise of Professional Development

No one can doubt the efficacy of conferences and seminars in general. These events are usually carefully planned and structured to present a wide selection of topics and experiences that cater to the needs and expectations of all participants. Unfortunately, the traditional one-time, one-size-fits-all seminar remains a preferred professional development model despite research indicating that it is ineffective (Bridges, 1993; Darling-Hammond, 1997; Darling-Hammond, 1998; Sparks, 2002). As Denis Sparks (2002) notes:

> [P]rofessional development as it is experienced by most teachers and
> principals is pretty much like it has always been—unfocused, insuf-
> ficient, and irrelevant to the day-to-day problems faced by frontline
> educators. Put another way, a great deal more is known today about
> good staff development than is regularly practiced in schools.
> (p. 14)

According to Haynes Mizell (2002), "high-quality staff development,
like the responsive classroom, needs to exemplify honored voice, a
collaborative construction of meaning, and a shared sense of knowing
between student and teacher" (p. 35). He goes on to explain that sustained, high-quality staff development can enhance teacher performance, and that such success can also help teachers raise their
expectations about themselves and their students.

Professional development strategies must promote the best practices identified by years of research in the field. According to Birman,
Desimone, Porter, and Garet (2000), professional development
should center on the pedagogical content knowledge of teachers (see
Chapter 1). For strategies to be truly effective, they must be sustain-
able over time, emphasize collegial and collaborative interaction, provide for shared decision-making, and offer coherence between theory
and practice. Of all these factors, sustainability over time is perhaps
the most crucial.

Usually, but not always, the teachers themselves decide which
presentations to attend at conferences or seminars. Either way, mere
attendance will not necessarily result in enhanced learning. Most of
these events are chaotic and overcrowded, and participants can find
it hard to focus on personal development goals while running from
one session to another.

Conference or seminar plans can be helpful in this regard (see Figure 8.1). As soon as a teacher knows that he will be attending a presentation, he should first take some time to review the program and conduct an Internet search on both the topics to be covered and the presenters' previous work. Next the teacher should determine what he hopes to gain from the event, either on his own or with assistance from colleagues.

Once objectives are established, the teacher should brainstorm ways to attain them, such as surveying materials at a conference exhibit, liaising with staff from other schools, or interviewing other attendees or presenters. The plan should allow for some scheduling flexibility, and may also include a "bonus" activity—that is, one that isn't necessarily related to the teacher's area of concern, but may provide him with a welcome break or explore relevant issues. For example, a teacher whose main area of concern is implementation of content standards for ESL students, but who is also interested in pursuing administrative opportunities in the future, may choose to attend a poster session on program administration. Bonus activities are supposed to be fun and provide relaxation from the busy schedule of a conference or course. In the case of extended workshops, participants may choose to have lunch away from the workshop site, visit a museum, or otherwise decompress from the day's activities.

Most conference programs offer an overwhelming variety of presentations, many of which are offered concurrently. After researching topics and presenters, participants should consider the pros and cons of each event. Many conferences offer "strands" of related presentations or "spotlight sessions" where hot topics are introduced and discussed. These are ideal forums for participants to learn about new developments in the field and spot emerging trends in the profession.

8.1 Sample Conference or Seminar Plan

Teacher: _____

Event: _____ **Date(s):** _____

Part 1. Plan

Personal goals (what do I expect to get from attending the event?):

_____

_____

_____

Means for attaining goals (what activities will I engage in during the event?):

Lectures _____

Workshops _____

Courses _____

Networking _____

Visits _____

Interviews _____

Bonus activity _____

Part 2. Evaluation

Summary of the event (What did I get out of attending the event?):

_____

_____

_____

Proposed follow-up to the event (What do I intend to do as a result of having attended the event?):

Objectives to Accomplish	Actions to Be Taken and by Whom	Resources Needed	Criteria for Success	Proposed Deadline for Follow-Up

During the conference, participants are encouraged to keep field notes (see Chapter 6). They should also keep a copy of their conference evaluation forms, as a reminder of their overall impressions. As soon as the event is finished, teachers should write up a summary of the presentations in which they evaluate the event and reflect on whether or not they achieved their initial goals. This reflective evaluation will form the basis of the teachers' reports to their schools. Teachers should have between one and two weeks to process all the experiences from the event before presenting their reports, during which time they can put their thoughts in order, select adequate materials to share, and plan a suitable presentation. They should take care to clearly specify the authors of any documents they present, as well as the time and date of the presentations discussed, and to write their own personal impressions on the handouts.

During these two weeks, teachers should complete the next section of the conference or seminar plan. Using all their materials from and reflections on the event, they should set objectives for sharing the lessons learned with the rest of the community—giving thought to the format, location, and resources needed for the report, as well as to their personal criteria for reporting successfully. Individual or collective rubrics, as suggested in Chapter 6, can help teachers keep their efforts to share learning with the community focused on the community's needs, while planning an interesting and engaging report.

Teachers can capitalize on the events they attend in a multitude of ways: they can develop action plans, implement a new teaching procedure they learned about, write a journal article, or contribute reflections to the school's Web page. According to Birman and colleagues (2000), "activities of longer duration have more subject-area content focus, more opportunities for active learning, and more coherence with teachers' other experiences than do shorter activities" (p. 3).

Conference or seminar plans are particularly suited to professionals who need incentives to renew their commitment to their careers. These professionals have attended many professional development events before, but may not have consciously focused on their own development needs. Conference or seminar plans can help teachers make more sense out of conferences and seminars while helping them feel that they too can contribute to the development of the school and profession. Plans are also powerful tools for novices, as they provide a safe structure for exploring new ideas and techniques while also supporting self-reflection and assessment.

– 9 –

Sharing Living Theories
to Help Others Develop

Ruth's Story (Epilogue)

In Chapter 8, I discussed how Ruth focused her participation in an
international conference by writing up a conference plan. This strategy led her to organize conference materials and communicate her
learning to others in the district. Soon, the district superintendent
encouraged her to develop a workshop based on her report for the
entire district. Because this would be Ruth's first professional presentation to a wide audience, she decided to review the principles of
effective in-service training. She read extensively on the topic of her
presentation, as well as on principles of adult learning. As she developed the format for the workshop, she asked for her colleagues' opinions and sent a survey of interests to potential workshop participants.
She used their answers to help inform the workshop's structure.

During the workshop, Ruth involved participants in active learning activities and provided them with a host of resources and suggestions for follow-up, including peer-to-peer coaching and collaborative

action research. She also demonstrated how she applied the ideas she'd learned at the conference in her own classroom, and reflected on their effects on her students' learning. At the end of the workshop, Ruth asked participants to evaluate it. She was happy to see that most comments were positive; more importantly, she discovered that she had become an expert in the topic and had learned how to design and deliver effective in-service training.

Research on the effectiveness of colleague-to-colleague workshops such as Ruth's is mixed. Guskey (2000) suggests that district-wide designs for such activities offer greater benefits than do site-based approaches, including opportunities to

- Perceive overarching themes beyond building issues (a necessary requirement of systemic reforms),
- Share resources and ideas with a wider segment of the teaching profession,
- Collaborate across school levels, and
- Share expertise more efficiently.

According to Bridges (1993):

The attribution to teachers of responsibility for their own professional development is presented and perceived both as a recognition of their extended professionalism and as a contribution to that extension. It fits comfortably with two decades of development which have provided a fertile range of possibilities for the expansion of teacher's roles as:

- Curriculum developers;
- Researchers—notably within the framework of classroom action research;
- Self-evaluators—within the context of school reviews and personal appraisal;
- Self-developers—either formally as advisory teachers or less formally as 'consultants' available to support development and training across schools. (p. 57)

In-house training should promote active engagement and reflection by all participants. As Pontz (2003) writes:

If training is to be effective and reasonably successful, it must at the very least:

- Be motivating, i.e. its objectives must be precise.
- Set goals that can actually be attained by individuals, providing a challenge though not an impossible one.
- Require the individual to draw upon knowledge she has already acquired—so that she does not feel lost—while at the same time enhancing it so that she has a sense of being able to reuse her knowledge in everyday life.
- Give the individual the opportunity to choose—so that she can exercise her newfound autonomy.
- Take place over a sufficient period of time, so that the learner's other occupations and obligations can be catered for.
- Lead to a final achievement, i.e. meet the goals initially set. (p. 165)

Teacher-led training should also emphasize the following principles (Burns, 1995; Knowles, Holton, & Swanson, 1998; Merriam & Caffarella, 1999):

- Optimal adult learning occurs when the information presented is adequately organized around the adult's previous knowledge and experience.
- Adult readiness to learn depends on the quantity and quality of prior knowledge and experience.
- Because each adult has a different quantity and quality of experience, each engages in learning from a distinct starting point.
- Adult educators must make their instruction practices meaningful by ensuring that they correspond to the experiential background of each learner in the class.
- The more meaningful the instructional activities and materials, the easier it will be for adults to learn.
- Instructional activities and materials should actively involve participants at the affective (feeling), cognitive (thinking), and psychomotor (doing) levels.

In addition to these principles, effective adult instruction should include the following three criteria:

1. **Direction** toward specific aims relevant to the learners' needs,
2. **Congruence** with the learners' prior experience and knowledge, and
3. **Multi-sensory and multi-dimensional engagement** of the learner.

Regarding the first criterion, direction, Pontz (2003) stresses that:

It is necessary from the outset to ensure that training has a precise objective and that there is a goal to be reached. Training must therefore provide for and lead to a final result, on the basis of which it will be possible to assess what has been achieved. In the same way, the objectives of training must be explicit and shown to be in line with the expectations of the learners. Training must take account of the social realities of the learners and the environment, so that learners are able to satisfy the specific desires they had when embarking upon the course. (p. 175)

As for congruence, Bridges (1993) describes the necessary connection between experience and learning activity as creating

[T]he conditions under which people . . . can be present in the same place at the same time, attending to the same events, and have totally different experiences. . . . Experience challenges our beliefs and we have, through our imagination and intelligence, to refine or adjust those beliefs to experience so that we are once more able to go about our business. (p. 61)

Burns (1995) emphasizes the importance of engagement to congruence, explaining that "active, rather than passive, participation in the learning activity enhances learning. Adults who are personally involved discover relationships, concepts and meaning as their own and are intrinsically rewarded. Adult educators who encourage active participation help to bring about more meaningful and permanent learning" (p. 255).

According to Jarvis (1987a; 1987b), the tensions between people's *biographies* and *experiences* are prerequisites for learning. As he puts it, the "inability to cope with the situation unthinkingly, instinctively, is at the heart of all learning" (1987a, p. 35). He contends that this tension leads to nine learning "paths" shown in Figure 9.1.

9.1 Jarvis's Hierarchy of Learning Experiences

Category	Experience	Characteristics
Nonlearning	Presumption	The individual responds mechanically to the experience.
	Nonconsideration	The individual is too concerned with other experiences to concentrate on this one.
	Rejection	The individual ignores the opportunity to learn.
Nonreflective	Preconscious	The individual unconsciously processes and internalizes the learning.
	Practice	The individual repeats the experience until it is learned.
	Memorization	The individual concentrates on the experience so that she can reproduce it later.
Higher-Order	Contemplation	The individual muses on the experience but does not respond behaviorally.
	Reflective practice	The individual engages in a process of performance similar to problem-solving.
	Experimental learning	The individual actively engages in experiences aimed at changing the present conditions of her teaching and learning environment.

Source: Adapted from Jarvis (1987a).

Delivering Presentations, Workshops, and Seminars

Most current professional development practices are in line with Jarvis's category of nonreflective learning—especially lectures, workshops, and seminars. It is possible, however, for these practices to result in higher forms of learning if they are approached from a more learner-focused perspective than usual.

Magestro and Stanford-Blair (2000) suggest a staff development template (Figure 9.2) that reveals the teacher-learners' motivations. According to the authors, "Effective staff development programs must offer small, but significant, doses of user-friendly, high-challenge, low-threat, and hands-on activities that encourage teachers to construct their own knowledge, to reflect on their practices, and to try out new approaches" (p. 35). To this end, they suggest that developers ask themselves the following questions, which stem from Wlodkowski and Ginsberg's (1995) work on diversity:

- Do the learners feel included?
- Does the module engender a positive attitude?
- Is the context meaningful?
- Do the activities help participants feel more competent?

Though the template in Figure 9.2 has proved extremely effective for a variety of professional development activities, it still assumes that the presenter makes most of the decisions, with the audience remaining at the receiving end. An alternative to this approach might be a more flexible planning model based on the specific needs and motivations of the participants, such as the 6-E approach to workshop design. This planning framework helps presenters peg their instruction to community-specific needs, using a variety of procedures to

9.2 Magestro and Stanford-Blair's Staff Development Template

Step 1: Identify the purpose and objectives of the meeting

What do you want participants to learn and be able to do as a result of this activity? Remember that the scope of the objective needs to fit the time allocated to the meeting.

Step 2: Select the resource(s) you plan to use as a basis for the activity

Content: Journal articles, books, videos, inquiry kits.
Process: Overhead transparencies, flip charts.

Step 3: Prepare an agenda that fits the timeframe available

Each agenda should include:

- **An activator.** An activity to elicit prior knowledge, beliefs, or attitudes.
- **Brief input.** Information drawn from the resources identified above and delivered through multiple modalities (visual, auditory, or kinesthetic).
- **Discussion.** Opportunities for participants to reflect on and respond to the input.
- **Activities.** Brain-compatible learning activities.
- **A summarizer.** An activity to elicit reflection on content and process.
- **Next steps.** Personal commitments to follow up with a new strategy or action research.

Step 4: Revisit or follow-up activities

Support strategies include peer planning, teaching, and coaching.

Source: Magestro and Stanford-Blair (2000, pp. 34–35).

facilitate the participants' encounter with new experiences. The six E's of the approach are: envisioning, explaining, enthusing, engaging, exploring, and empowering.

Envisioning. When schools decide to undergo training, they appoint a workshop coordinator—someone whom staff members perceive as possessing the knowledge and skills that they lack. Working together, the staff and the coordinator analyze the needs served by and outcomes expected from the workshop. If the staff is not knowledgeable enough to provide input, the workshop coordinator should specify outcomes while keeping staff members informed and requesting their approval before moving on.

As an example, I was recently contacted by the Association of Middle School Principals (AMSP) to deliver a two-day workshop on the role of the principal as academic leader. Because meeting with all potential workshop participants was impossible, I decided to send them a survey of their needs via e-mail (see Figure 9.3). I then used the completed surveys to design suitable outcomes for the workshop.

Explaining. Once the intended outcomes have been clearly specified, the workshop coordinator should decide, with the help of the participants, on suitable evidence of success in judging the eventual outcomes. This can be done by means of an individually or collectively constructed rubric, or by using a workshop assessment questionnaire. Involving the participants will ensure that the workshop is in line with their needs and provide them with a clear focus, thus maximizing their understanding, participation, and motivation.

The coordinator should also present potential materials and resources for use in the workshop at this stage, and ask potential participants for their thoughts. Prior to conducting the AMSP workshop, I presented participants with an annotated list of books and articles and asked them to select those that they found most suitable for their needs. I also asked them to select their favorite interactive strategies from the ones listed in Question 5 of Figure 9.3.

9.3 Sample E-Mail Needs Survey

Dear Colleagues,

I am thrilled to be working with you on this project. In order for this workshop to be truly effective, I would appreciate your devoting some time to answering the questions in this survey. When you do so, please hit the "respond to all" button on your e-mail, so that everyone can see everyone else's responses.

   Thank you for your time and interest in this topic. I look forward to hearing from you all.

                              Kindest regards,
                              Gabriel

Survey

1. Why have you chosen to participate in this professional development activity?

_____

_____

_____

2. What topics would you like to explore in the workshop?

_____

_____

_____

3. Are there any other topics you would like to explore?

_____

_____

_____

4. What questions do you have about the workshop?

_____

_____

_____

(cont.)

9.3 Sample E-Mail Needs Survey (*cont.*)

5. Please indicate the percentage of total time you would like to devote to each of the following interactive activities during the workshop:

     a. Mini-lectures by the workshop coordinator   _____ percent of the time
     b. Small-group discussion of readings   _____ percent of the time
     c. Case study analysis   _____ percent of the time
     d. Group problem-solving   _____ percent of the time
     e. Simulations/role-plays   _____ percent of the time
     f. Video demonstrations   _____ percent of the time
     g. Live demonstrations   _____ percent of the time
     h. Debate   _____ percent of the time
     i. Games   _____ percent of the time

6. What do you expect to know and be able to do at the end of this workshop?

_____

_____

_____

7. How will we know whether we have achieved the outcomes of this workshop?

_____

_____

_____

8. If this workshop were EXCELLENT, what would it look like?

_____

_____

_____

9. If this workshop were VERY GOOD, what would it look like?

_____

_____

_____

10. If this workshop were ACCEPTABLE, what would it look like?

_____

_____

_____

Enthusing. Having clearly specified outcomes and suitable evidence, the workshop coordinator should now begin planning the activity. The purpose of this stage is to illustrate for the participants the topics to be covered in the workshop—by using brain maps and other advanced organizers, having participants brainstorm their initial understanding of the topic, or simply promoting small-group discussion on the topic.

I have found that starting off with a prompt that strongly conveys a common concern among the participants is a good motivator. In the case of the AMSP workshop, I began by displaying cartoons of principals in everyday situations, which tallied with the concerns participants had listed in the e-mail survey. I then asked everyone to stand up as I displayed each cartoon with an overhead projector, and to sit down if they had "been there, done that." By the third cartoon, all the principals were sitting. This exercise provided participants with a strong sense of mutual concern and a common focus for the rest of the workshop.

Engaging. At this stage of the workshop, participants should engage in "loop input activities." Woodward (1993) uses this term to describe situations in which participants experience a theory by engaging in activities that exemplify it. These loop input activities should fulfill two objectives: to make the theoretical principles explicit, and to promote high levels of interaction among participants.

During the AMSP workshop, we discussed Heron's Six Category Intervention Analysis (Heron, 1990). In order to promote understanding and engagement, I prepared situational cue cards and distributed them to participants, who worked in pairs to devise suitable interventions for the problems presented. When the exercise was completed, the group reconvened to share the results. Heron's model was then used as a prompt for reflecting on the efficacy of the interventions. Finally, participants exchanged cue cards and went over the simulation again.

Exploring. During this phase of the workshop, participants should team up with peers to pursue collaborative development activities related to the workshop's content.

It is important that participants draft action plans during the workshop, with the facilitator's assistance if necessary, so that there is some continuity to the development process. The ultimate purpose of the exploring stage is to provide participants with "executive control"—the transfer of the strategies to the teacher's actual teaching repertoire (Joyce & Showers, 1995).

Empowering. The last phase of the 6-E approach is a follow-up to the previous two stages, and involves assessing the effect of the workshop on teacher and student learning. For example, participants can begin by reflecting on a rubric constructed during the explaining phase, following which they can create portfolio presentations to share their evidence of development during the workshop, assess the workshop and its facilitator, and conduct statistical analyses of student performance since the teacher's participation in the workshop. Information gathered during the empowering stage should be systematized, shared with as wide an audience as possible, and serve as the basis for future diagnoses of needs and for planning future development strategies. The fact that this stage occurs only after participants have had a chance to explore the workshop content through sustained teaching and learning activities adds an extra measure of validity to the evaluation.

Figure 9.4 summarizes the 6-E approach to workshop development.

9.4 The 6-E Experiential Approach to Workshop Design

INTO	**Envisioning**	• Assess development needs • Appoint workshop coordinator(s) • Specify outcomes
	Explaining	• Specify evidence of outcomes achievement • Explore potential resources
THROUGH	**Enthusing**	• Develop a sequence of activities • Provide an overview of the workshop contents
	Engaging	• Provide active learning opportunities • Engage in loop-input activities
BEYOND	**Exploring**	• Apply workshop ideas to the classroom • Engage in other collaborative development strategies
	Empowering	• Assess the workshop's effect on teachers, students, and the school community • Apply assessment data to future professional development activities

Extended Professional Development Courses

The 6-E approach can be used for planning, implementing, and evaluating workshops as well as more extended professional development courses. The three most popular methods of extended-course delivery are self-directed learning, self-paced learning, and contract learning. According to Burns (1995), self-directed learning

- Is motivating, because it is derived from real-life needs;
- Helps people develop and consolidate research skills;
- Helps people learn how to apply new learning to real-life problems;
- Is particularly useful for large populations with diverse needs; and
- Allows learners to select the content and process of learning themselves.

By these standards, the 6-E approach can be considered a self-directed learning activity in that it not only fosters learning autonomy, but also presents participants with varied options that they can complete at their own pace.

By contrast, Burns describes self-paced learning as

[T]he provision in the structure of the learning activity that allows the learners to work through the material at their own pace. A major element in the delivery of self-directed education and training for adults in the workplace is self-paced learning. . . . Self-pacing develops independence and helps those whose gradually deteriorating speed of operation of the nervous system—in other words, aging populations—would impede their performance if required to keep up to a fixed speed. (1995, p. 260)

Because they do not impose time constraints on participants, the collaborative strategies of the Teacher's Choice Framework tally with the self-paced learning philosophy and, more directly, with contract learning. Burns describes contract learning as a method in which learners "write their own objectives, determine what work is to be done, what resources are to be used and design the evaluation criteria. The learner *owns* the learning project—this provides the motivation to see it through" (pp. 262–263). Contract learning is the method upon which the Teacher's Choice Framework rests, in that it provides teachers with a user-friendly way to plan and direct their own professional learning. Teachers need to work together to plan their development efforts based on their needs and knowledge. In the Teacher's Choice Framework, the professional development profile shown in Chapter 2, Figure 2.5, serves as a learning contract.

The choice of delivery method is, as always, determined by the specific needs of the learners. No matter what method is ultimately chosen, course activities should be both collaborative and congruent with adult learning principles. Traditional lectures with little or no participant involvement should be avoided; instead, course developers should consider more interactive strategies, such as those shown in Figure 9.5.

9.5 Collaborative Learning Activities for Extended Courses

Activity	Purpose	Description
Mini-Lecture	*To present facts, content, and information*	A brief presentation (not more than 15 minutes) of key issues. Participants can take notes during the lecture and provide a summary via work in *buzz groups* (see below).
Demonstration	*To show how a skill is performed*	A careful, step-by-step explication of the stages in performance of a skill. The demonstration should flow naturally but slowly enough for participants to understand each step.
Case studies	*To promote analysis and problem-solving*	Thorough but unfinished data about a situation familiar to participants, who analyze and explain the data in light of their knowledge and experience.
Brainstorming	*To explore participants' knowledge*	Participants provide ideas about a topic, being sure to write everything down (quantity before quality). Following this, they prioritize and synthesize their notes (quality before quantity).

(cont.)

9.5 Collaborative Learning Activities for Extended Courses (*cont.*)

Activity	Purpose	Description
Buzz Groups	*To allow participants to elaborate content*	Participants gather in groups of four or five to synthesize their understanding and exchange opinions.
Discussion	*To engage participants in voicing their opinions*	Participants freely interact with one another to assess alternative opinions on a topic or skill. Following this, they reflect on areas of agreement.
Socratic Questioning	*To structure participants' thinking towards the discovery of patterns*	The facilitator carefully structures a series of questions aimed at guiding participants' reasoning through dialogue in order to help them spot patterns.
Debates	*To provide reflective assessment of opposing point of view*	Participants are divided into opposing opinion groups, which take turns presenting their views on a topic. Questions from each of the groups ensue. The aim is to extend the argument.
Panels	*To help participants weigh options*	Participants are divided into panelists and audience. Panelists present a specific area of the topic, following which the audience asks questions.
Projects	*To promote active problem-solving and application*	Participants develop a concrete outcome based on their understanding of and reflection on a topic.
Simulations	*To engage participants in contemplating issues from alternative perspectives*	Participants are assigned a role that they have to perform while interacting with other participants to solve a problem, reach a conclusion, or explore a concept.
Seminars	*To develop participants' expertise and reflection*	Each participant is assigned an area of a topic in which to specialize. Participants research that area and present their conclusions to the rest of the group.

– 10 –

The Administrator's Role

We shouldn't try to do something better until we first determine if we should do it at all.

—Dwight D. Eisenhower

Administrators are like lookouts on a ship: their positions allow them to perceive their surroundings from a more global perspective than that of teachers busy with day-to-day classroom events. By keeping their sights on the horizon, administrators help provide teachers with direction for their actions.

In addition to their lookout work, administrators serve as professional development managers, defined by Bradley, Kallick, and Regan (1991) as those who create "a well-ordered environment so that work can be accomplished effectively and efficiently to the satisfaction of those involved" (p. 5). When approaching professional development from the perspective of teachers' personal agendas, they act as catalysts of teacher growth and development; when they single-handedly make decisions on behalf of teachers, they render them disempowered. Administrators need to ensure that development strategies help manage teachers' intentions. Just as it is vital for administrators to ensure that the necessary conditions for teacher learning to thrive are in place, an orderly environment is essential for the satisfaction of all involved: by helping teachers organize the strategies they pursue, administrators provide a safe and orderly environment for learning to happen.

According to Bradley and colleagues (1991), administrators have two main duties—making their knowledge accessible to staff and acting as intermediaries—and three main management styles:

1. **Autocratic.** Administrators who adopt this management style can make decisions—especially regarding brief, low-risk tasks—quickly. However, this approach does not help build morale or a sense of community. The administrator makes decisions by himself with little or no input from others; information does not generally flow freely and faulty decisions can often be made. This kind of management is characteristic of a traditional approach to professional development, and has no place in the Teacher's Choice Framework.
2. **Laissez-faire.** This style of management requires administrators to be highly creative and naturally independent. However, because their interactions often lack a clear focus, and because it can take so long for teachers to make decisions, this style is not particularly effective.
3. **Democratic.** This is the management style best suited for the Teacher's Choice Framework, as it requires managers to consult staff and make decisions based on their needs and expectations. Though this consultation process may be time-consuming, it results in enhanced morale and commitment and more effective decisions.

Good administrators are providers, facilitators, communicators, organizers, and evaluators of professional development. Because of their organizational leadership functions, they are instrumental in providing faculty with expert help—and when they can't, they should arrange for it to be provided. They should also provide staff with release time or opportunities for them to exercise their professional leadership.

Administrators also facilitate contact among colleagues in the building, and even across schools and districts. To borrow a term from Richard Sagor, every administrator serves as a "critical friend" to teachers—that is, as "a person who has [their] interest at heart and gives [them] constructive criticism" (1992, p. 46). This role is closely linked to the administrator's main task of helping create a school climate conducive to teacher learning and student success.

Administrators should communicate to the wider school community all relevant information that touches on professional development, including data on how to better implement strategies, teacher's needs and expectations about student learning and their own professional development, news from the field, and most importantly, success stories from the community. All administrators should be good inquirers and advisors as well as good listeners.

Administrators should also organize time and resources effectively, by systematizing teacher interaction, adopting flexible schedules, providing networking opportunities, and meeting with teachers on a regular (and individual) basis to collaborate on planning, monitoring, and evaluating their efforts. Recordkeeping, such as shown in Figure 10.1, is crucial to these meetings. Thorough notes help administrators track the professional development of teachers and can be used to document different strategies and results. Notice that in the template in Figure 10.1, teachers can choose to participate in meetings with administrators either alone or accompanied by critical friends, coaches, or mentors.

Figure 10.2 summarizes the main roles of administrators in a professional development program.

Evaluation

Evaluation should not be left for administrators alone, nor should it be only a concluding activity. It is an integral component of any professional development process, and as such must be congruent with the needs, expectations, and outcomes desired of all involved.

Kerry (1993) notes that it's "becoming increasingly difficult to pursue a policy of linking in-service training with classroom practice directly" (p. 176)—a concern that has not gone unnoticed over the past few years. Given the asynchronous effect of professional development programs on student learning, evaluating their results can seem too daunting and complex. Yet evaluation can be as important as teacher involvement in professional development.

Clearly, evaluation of professional development should not be confused with evaluation of teachers; indeed, results of the latter are one source of data among the many that contribute to accurate program assessment. One of the most frequently cited models of professional development evaluation was devised by Donald Kirkpatrick (Champion, 2002). According to this model, programs are assessed based on four criteria:

1. Reaction of participants to the program model and procedures.
2. Learning that results from engagement in the program.
3. Use of the knowledge gained in the program.
4. Results of students' learning.

10.1 Professional Development Meeting Record

Teacher: _____ **Subject/Grade:** _____

Administrator: _____ **Others present:** _____

Professional development strategies chosen:

1. _____

    Mandated training on strategy completed on: _____

2. _____

    Mandated training on strategy completed on: _____

Reasons for teacher's choice of strategies:

_____

_____

Expected outcomes:

_____

_____

Timeline of activities:

Aug.	Sept.	Oct.	Nov.	Dec.	Jan.	Feb.	Mar.	Apr.	May

Important dates:

_____   _____

_____   _____

_____   _____

_____   _____

(cont.)

10.1 Professional Development Meeting Record (*cont.*)

Summary of meetings:

Planning meeting
Date: _____ Participants: _____

_____
_____

Monitoring meeting
Date: _____ Participants: _____

_____
_____

Evaluative meeting
Date: _____ Participants: _____

_____
_____

Teacher's self-assessment:

_____
_____
_____
_____

Peer assessment:

_____
_____
_____
_____

Next steps:

_____
_____
_____
_____
_____

(*cont.*)

10.1 Professional Development Meeting Record (*cont.*)

Additional notes and comments:

_____

Teacher's signature   **Administrator's signature**   **Date**

These four components serve as triggers to collect and organize information pertaining to the efficacy of the professional development program. Information on participants' reactions is usually gleaned from surveys; data on teacher learning can be assessed through formal tests, or via supervision following the program. Teachers' use of knowledge gained in the program can also be assessed via supervision. Finally, results of students' learning can be evaluated using standardized tests. Once information has been gathered for each of the components of the model, it is contrasted with the other three.

10.2 Roles and Functions of Administrators

Role	Functions
Provider	• Provides mandatory professional development training • Offers "expert" help, advice, and guidance • Grants release time and opportunities for growth • Presents data to guide teacher efforts
Facilitator	• Promotes contact among colleagues by helping them spot suitable collaborators • Serves as a critical friend to teachers • Offers resources at the school, district, state, or national level • Helps create a climate conducive to teacher learning
Communicator	• Provides data on teaching and learning • Pays attention to stakeholders' needs and expectations • Promotes effective professional development practices • Serves as a good advisor, inquirer, and listener • Maintains an archive of the school's professional development history • Shares professional development "success stories" with other schools and districts
Organizer	• Organizes meetings for faculty to share their development stories • Convenes individual meetings with teachers to plan, monitor, and evaluate their professional development • Encourages interaction among participants in the professional development process • Celebrates the successes of teachers and students
Evaluator	Assesses professional development cycles and strategies, teacher performance, and use of resources

Guskey (2000) expands on Kirkpatrick's model by adding a fifth criterion: organizational support and change. Good evaluations, Guskey notes, are "the product of thoughtful planning, the ability to ask good questions, and a basic understanding about how to find valid answers. In many ways, they are simply the refinement of everyday thinking. Good evaluations provide information that is sound, meaningful, and sufficiently reliable to use in making thoughtful and responsible decisions about professional development processes and effects" (1998).

Kerry (1993) distinguishes between summative and formative evaluation:

> At the formative end of this spectrum the concern may be to define or describe quality processes rather than 'measure' outcomes. Oldroyd and Hall (1991) go further and identify four kinds of quality control for professional development:
>
> • **Monitoring.** Are we carrying out our plans?
>
> • **Formative evaluation.** Do we need to adjust our plans and how are we carrying them out?
>
> • **Summative evaluation.** Was the process successful and were the outcomes worthwhile and valuable?
>
> • **Review.** Should we change our assumptions, aims, priorities and approach? (p. 166)

By contrast, the Teacher's Choice Framework offers an evaluation model comprising four distinct stages: planning, suitability assessment, evaluation, and effect.

Stage 1: Planning

This phase takes place before the professional development event begins, and allows teachers to explore their needs and awareness levels. Its purpose is to help teachers and administrators understand the outcomes necessary for success. During this phase, teachers and administrators reflect on the suitability of different strategies and assessment measures. In evaluating the planning stage, administrators might use the following guiding questions:

- Where are we now?
- Where do we need to go?
- Why do we need to go there?
- How do we get there from here?
- How do we know whether this will work?

Evaluative data at this stage can include the following:

- Interviews with students, parents, and faculty;
- Results from standardized tests;
- Degree to which teaching reflects district, state, and national standards;
- Classroom observation of faculty;
- Surveys of teacher needs or expectations;
- Anecdotal records; and
- Communications between the school and the community, teachers and parents, teachers and administrators.

These data should lay the groundwork for a thorough needs analysis, which should in turn result in an initial set of desired outcomes.

Stage 2: Suitability Assessment

The purpose of this stage is to provide direction and ongoing feedback on the necessary congruence among outcomes, activities, and the teachers' individual development plans. Guiding questions for this phase include:

- How are we doing?
- How do we know this?
- What needs fixing, changing, or suppressing, and why?

The fundamental data for this stage are participants' opinions about the different collaborative development strategies, each of which contains an evaluative component that can provide a timely indication of necessary changes. Data can be collected via interviews, surveys, questionnaires, and analysis of student progress, as well as through analysis of tools such as journals or portfolios. Rubrics, too, can be particularly helpful at this stage, as their differentiated nature allows stakeholders to clearly see where changes need to be made; those based on research-based standards, such as the ones issued by the National Staff Development Council, can provide guidance.

Another option is to establish an assessment committee in charge of charting the progress of the learning community towards the intended outcomes. This committee, made up of faculty-selected members, serves as an objective outside assessor of each strategy's effectiveness. In order to act with adequate direction, the committee should have a set of guidelines to safeguard its objectivity. Kushner (2000) suggests that committee members ask themselves the following questions:

- Why are you investigating? On whose behalf?
- How, in general, do you see your status in relation to those you observe—higher, lower, different, more/less privileged? What difference does it make?
- Do you believe what your respondents say to you, in general, and if you do, how and why do you believe them? (For example, do you distinguish the truth value of what people say to you

according to their place in the power structure, according to their age, their class, their gender, whether you like them or not?)

- Can you conduct an investigation with people you do not like (that is, and still be fair and rigorous)?

- How do you balance your obligations/loyalties to the institutions involved (including your own) with those towards the individuals who live in the institutions implied by your investigation? (For example, if there is a tension between fairness to an individual and protecting the stability of a democratic institution, which are you prepared to sacrifice?)

- Who owns the data you collect? If you, what do you do with it after the enquiry—if not you, what are you doing with it in the first place? (p. 79)

Stage 3: Evaluation

This phase occurs when teachers complete their professional development cycle, and constitutes an initial judgment of the strategies' effectiveness. The focus at this stage should be on the overall effectiveness both of the professional development plan and of particular development strategies. There are two key questions in Stage 3: "Have we reached our destination?" and "How do we know?"

Data that can help answer these questions include the following:

- Records of student progress
- Student test scores
- Student work in general
- Interviews with students and parents
- Professional development products such as portfolios and new curricula and materials

- Faculty self-assessments
- Administrator evaluations of teacher performance
- Reports from coaches, coordinators, mentors, or professional development providers

For evaluative criteria to prove the success of a development plan or strategy, they should point to improved teaching and student learning and a narrowing of student achievement gaps (Champion, 2002). Retrospectively analyzing the questions posed at each phase of the evaluation process may help obtain such data.

Stage 4: Effect

In the final evaluative phase, administrators assess the effect of the professional development plan. Of course, this can only occur once the original development plan is completed—during the academic year, for instance. Teachers and administrators should ask the following questions at this stage:

- How accurate were our initial evaluation claims?
- How do we know?
- Where do we go from here?

Student and teacher evaluation data, perceptions from the broader community, and objective records of teacher and student performance can all be used to assess the effect of the strategies implemented so far. It is important that this information feed back into current development plans in order to enhance them.

Ultimately, the most important information to be gleaned at this stage of the evaluation process is the degree to which development has affected student learning outcomes. As Guskey (2000) notes, this information

- Offers new perspectives on old problems,
- Promotes high expectations and more rigorous standards,
- Broadens perspectives on the factors that influence professional development, and
- Empowers professional developers to make what they do count.

Finally, it is important to communicate evaluation results for the benefit of all involved. Developing case studies and sharing them through publications can help school leaders construct school-specific knowledge that they can modify and apply to different situations. (See Figure 10.3 for a diagram summarizing the data collection process.)

Summary

In this chapter we reviewed the administrator's role in supporting the development needs of every faculty member for the benefit of all learners. We also discussed the Teacher's Choice Framework model for evaluating professional development, which provides communities with a flexible format for assessing their efforts on an ongoing basis, enabling them to focus on narrowing the achievement gap of all students.

Evaluation helps better orient teachers and students alike to the future. As Paulo Freire (1996) explains:

The future is not a province some distance from the present which just waits for us to arrive some day and perform the operation of

10.3 The Teacher's Choice Framework Evaluation Process

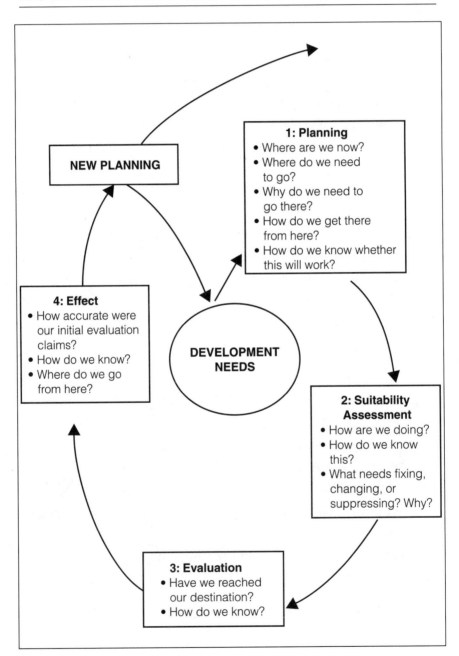

adding this ready-made tomorrow to today, which both becomes old and obsolete. The future is born of the present, from possibilities in contradiction, from the battle waged by forces that dialectically oppose each other. For this reason, as I always insist, the future is not a given fact, but a fact in progress. (p. 152)

References

Academy for Educational Development. (1985). *Teacher development in schools: A report to the Ford Foundation*. New York: Author.

Allchin, D. (1998). *Teaching as scholarly activity*. Available: http://www.utep.edu/~cetal/portfoli/profess.htm.

Armstrong, J. L., & Yarbrough, S. L. (1996). Group learning: The role of the environment. *New Directions for Adult and Continuing Education, 71*, 33–39.

Barker, K., Kagan, D., Klemp, R., Roderick, S., & Takenaga-Taga, D. (1997). *Toward a growth model of teacher professionalism*. Available: http://www.teachnet.org/TNPI/research/network/lafellows.htm.

Barone, T. E. (1998). Aesthetic dimensions of supervision. In G. R. Firth & E. F. Pajak (Eds.), *Handbook of research on school supervision*. New York: Simon & Schuster Macmillan.

Belbin, R. M. (1981). *Management teams: Why they succeed or fail*. London: Heinemann.

Bereiter, C. (2002). *Education and mind in the knowledge age*. Mahwah, NJ: Lawrence Erlbaum and Associates.

Birchak, B., Connor, C., Crawford, K., Kahn, L., Kayer, S., Turner, S., & Short, K. (1998). *Teacher study groups: Building community through dialogue and reflection*. Urbana, IL: National Council of Teachers of English.

Birman, B., Desimone, L., Porter, A., & Garet, M. (2000). Designing professional development that works. *Educational Leadership, 57*(8), 28–33.

Blythe, T., Allen, D., & Schieffelin Powell, B. (1999). *Looking together at student work: A companion guide to assessing student learning*. New York: Teachers College Press.

Boss, S. (2000). Great expectations: Making a career of teaching. *NW Education Magazine 5*(4), 1–6.

Bradley, M. J., Kallick, B. O., & Regan, H. B. (1991). *The staff development manager: A guide to professional growth*. Needham Heights, MA: Allyn and Bacon.

Bredo, E. (1997). The social construction of learning. In Gary D. Phye (Ed.), *Handbook of academic learning: Construction of knowledge*. San Diego, CA: Academic Press.

Bridges, D. (1993). School-based teacher education. In D. Bridges and T. Kerry (Eds.), *Developing teachers professionally: Reflection for initial and in-service trainers* (pp. 51–66). London: Routledge.

Brinton, D. M., Holter, C. A., & Goodwin, J. M. (1993). *Responding to dialogue journals in teacher preparation: What's effective?* Available: http://www.ncela.gwu.edu/miscpubs/tesol/tesoljournal/respondi.htm.

Brison, K., & Leavitt, S. (1999). *Guidelines for field notes and journals*. Available: http://www.union.edu/PUBLIC/ANTDEPT/fiji99/assignments/wk1notes.htm.

Brookfield, S. D. (1986). *Understanding and facilitating adult learning*. San Francisco: Jossey-Bass.

Brooks, V., & Sikes, P. (1997). *The good mentor guide: Initial teacher education in secondary schools*. Buckingham, England: Open University Press.

Bullock, A. A., & Hawk, P. P. (2001). *Professional teaching portfolios for practicing teachers*. Bloomington, IN: Phi Delta Kappa Educational Foundation.

Burns, R. (1995). *The adult learner at work: A comprehensive guide to the context, psychology, and methods of learning in the workplace*. Sydney: Business and Professional Publishing.

Butler, K. (1984). *Learning and teaching style in theory and practice*. Columbia, CT: The Learner's Dimension.

Carruthers, J. (1993). The principles and practice of mentoring. In B. Caldwell, & Carter M. A. (Eds.), *The return of the mentor: Strategies for workplace learning*. London: Falmer Press.

Champion, R. (2002). Taking measure: Choose the right data for the job. *Journal of Staff Development, 23*(3). Available: http://www.nsdc.org/library/jsd/champion233.html.

Cogan, M. L. (1973). *Clinical supervision*. Boston: Houghton Mifflin.

Cohen, E. (1994). *Designing group work: Strategies for the heterogeneous classroom* (2nd ed.). New York: Teachers College Press.

Cohen, L., & Manion, L. (2000). Action research. In L. Cohen, L. Manion, & K. Morrison (Eds.), *Research methods in education* (5th ed.). London: Routledge-Falmer.

Costa, A., & Garmston, R. (2002). *Cognitive coaching: A foundation for renaissance schools*. Norwood, IL: Christopher Gordon.

Cranton, P. (1996, Fall). Types of group learning. *New Directions for Adult and Continuing Education, 71*, 25–32.

Danielson, C. (1996). *Enhancing professional practice: A framework for teaching*. Alexandria, VA: Association for Supervision and Curriculum Development.

Darling-Hammond, L. (1997). *Doing what matters most: Investing in quality teaching*. New York: National Commission on Teaching and America's Future.

Darling-Hammond, L. (1998). Teacher learning that supports student learning. *Educational Leadership, 55*(5), 6–11.

Dewey, J. (1938/1997). *Experience and education*. New York: Touchstone. (Original work published 1938)

Díaz-Maggioli, G. (1996). The good, the bad and the ugly: Learning preferences in ESL. *English Teaching Forum, 34*(2), 32–39.

Díaz-Maggioli, G. (in press). Options in teacher professional development. *English Teaching Forum, 41*(2).

Doolittle, P. (1994). *Teacher portfolio assessment*. Washington, DC: ERIC Clearinghouse on Assessment and Evaluation. (ERIC Document Reproduction Service No. ED 385 608)

Doyle, M., & Straus, D. (1982). *The new interaction method: How to make meetings work*. New York: Jove.

Drennon, C., & Foucar-Szocki, D. (1996, Fall). Developing practitioner inquiry communities. *New Directions for Adult and Continuing Education, 71*, 25–32.

Du Bois, W. E. B. (1953). *The souls of black folk*. New York: Fawcett.

Eisner, E. W. (1982). An artistic approach to supervision. In T. Sergiovanni (Ed.), *Supervision of teaching*. Alexandria, VA: Association for Supervision and Curriculum Development.

English, L. (1999). An adult-learning approach to preparing mentors and mentees. *Mentoring & Tutoring, 7*(3), 195–201.

Federman Stein, R., & Hurd, S. (2000). *Using student teams in the classroom: A faculty guide*. Boston: Anker Publishing Company Inc.

Fessler, R., & Christensen, J. C. (1992). *The teacher career cycle: Understanding and guiding the professional development of teachers*. Boston: Allyn and Bacon.

Fletcher, S. (2000). *Mentoring in schools: A handbook of good practice*. London: Kogan Page.

Freire, P. (1970). *Pedagogy of the oppressed*. New York: Continuum.

Freire, P. (1996). *Letters to Cristina: Reflections on my life and work*. New York: Routledge.

Freire, P. (1998). *Pedagogy of freedom: Ethics, democracy and civic courage*. Lanham, MD: Rowman and Littlefield.

Frid, I. (1994). *I Ching*. Buenos Aires: Troquel.

Furlong, J., & Maynard, T. (1995). *Mentoring student teachers: The growth of professional knowledge*. London: Routledge.

Galbraith, P., & Anstrom, K. (1991). Peer coaching: An effective staff development model for educators of linguistically and culturally diverse students. *Directions in Language and Education, 1*(3), 1–6.

Garman, N. (1982). The clinical approach to supervision. In T. J. Sergiovanni (Ed.), *Supervision of teaching*. Alexandria, VA: Association for Supervision and Curriculum Development.

Glanz, J. (2000). Supervision: Don't discount the value of the modern. In J. Glanz and L. S. Behar-Horenstein (Eds.), *Paradigm debates in curriculum and supervision*. Westport, CT: Bergin & Garvey.

Goldhammer, R. (1969). *Clinical Supervision: Special methods for the supervision of teachers*. New York: Holt, Rinehart & Winston.

Goldsberry, L. (1986). Is clinical supervision practical? In W. J. Smyth (Ed.), *Learning about teaching through clinical supervision*. London: Falmer Press.

Granade Sullivan, C. (1997). Is staff development supervision? Yes. In J. Glanz and R. Neville (Eds.), *Educational supervision: Perspectives, issues and controversies*. Norwood, MA: Christopher Gordon Publishers.

Griffin, G. (1997). Is staff development supervision? No. In J. Glanz and R. Neville (Eds.), *Educational supervision: Perspectives, issues and controversies*. Norwood, MA: Christopher Gordon Publishers.

Griffiths, M., & Tann, S. (1992). Using reflective practice to link personal and public theories. *Journal of Education for Teaching, 18*(1), 69–84.

Grossman, J. (1990). *The making of a teacher.* New York: Teachers College Press.

Guskey, T. A. (1998). Evaluation must become an integral part of staff development. *Journal of Staff Development, 19*(4). Avaliable: http://www.nsdc.org/library/jsd/guskey194.html.

Guskey, T. A. (2000). *Evaluating professional development.* Thousand Oaks, CA: Corwin Press.

Hale, R. (1999). The dynamics of mentoring relationships: Towards an understanding of how mentoring supports learning. *Continuing Professional Development, 3.* Available: http://staff.bath.ac.uk/edssjf/dynamicsof.htm.

Hargreaves, A. (1994). *Changing teachers, changing times.* London: Cassell.

Haugen, L. (1998). *Writing a teaching philosophy.* Available: http://www.cte.iastate.edu/portfolio/philtip.html.

Hawkey, K. (1997). Roles, responsibilities, and relationships: A literature review and agenda for research. *Journal of Teacher Education, 48*(5), 325–333.

Haynes Mizell, M. (2002). *Shooting for the sun: The message of middle school reform.* New York: The Edna McConnell Clark Foundation.

Heron, J. (1990). *Helping the client: A practical guide.* London: Sage Publications.

Hills, H. (2001). *Team-based learning.* Burlington, VT: Gower Publishing Limited.

Huberman, M. (1989). *La vie des enseignants: Èvolution et Bilan d'une profession.* Neûchatel, Switzerland: Delachaux.

Jacob, G. M., Power, M. A., & Wan Inn, L. (2002). *The teacher's sourcebook for cooperative learning: Practical techniques, basic principles and frequently asked questions.* Thousand Oaks, CA: Corwin Press.

Jarvis, P. (1987a). *Adult learning in the social context.* London: Croom Helms.

Jarvis, P. (1987b). Meaningful and meaningless experience: Toward an analysis of learning from life. *Adult Education Quarterly, 37*(3), 164–172.

Johnson, B. (1993). *Teacher-as-researcher.* Washington, DC: ERIC Clearinghouse on Teacher Education. (ERIC Document Reproduction Service No. ED 355 205)

Johnson, D. W., & Johnson, R. T. (1984). Cooperative small-group learning. *Curriculum report, 14*(1) 2–7.

Joyce, B., & Showers, B. (1995). *Student achievement through staff development: Fundamentals of school renewal* (2nd ed.). New York: Longman.

Kagan, S. (1994). *Cooperative learning.* San Clemente, CA: Kagan Publishing.

Kerry, T. (1993). Evaluating INSET: The search for quality. In D. Bridges & T. Kerry (Eds.), *Developing teachers professionally: Reflection for initial and in-service trainers* (pp. 165–177). London: Routledge.

Knapper, C., & Wright, W. A. (2001, Winter). Using portfolios to document good teaching: Premises, purposes, practices. *New Directions for Teaching and Learning, 88,* 19–29.

Knowles, M., Holton, E., & Swanson, R. (1998). *The adult learner.* Houston, TX: Gulf Publishing.

Kushner, S. (2000). *Personalizing evaluation.* London: Sage Publications.

Lave, J. (1990). The culture of acquisition and practice of understanding. In J. W. Stigler, R. A. Shweder, & G. Herdt (Eds.), *Cultural psychology.* Cambridge: Cambridge University Press.

Le Compte, M., & Schensul, J. (1999). *Analyzing and interpreting ethnographic data.* Walnut Creek, CA: Altamira Press.

Lofland, J. (1995). *Analyzing social settings: A guide to quality observation and analysis* (3rd ed.). Belmont, CA: Wadsworth.

Lunt, N., Bennett, Y., McKenzie, P., & Powell, L. (1992). Understanding mentoring. *The Vocational Aspect of Education, 44*(1), 135–141.

Magestro, P., & Stanford-Blair, N. (2000). A tool for meaningful staff development. *Educational Leadership, 57*(8), 34–35.

Marczely, B. (2001). *Supervision in education: A differentiated approach with legal perspectives.* Gaithersburg, MD: Aspen Publishers, Inc.

McTaggart, R. (1997). *Participatory action research: International contexts and consequences.* Albany, NY: SUNY Press.

Merriam, S., & Caffarella, R. (1999). *Learning in adulthood: A comprehensive guide* (2nd ed.). San Francisco: Jossey-Bass.

Millwater, J., & Yarrow, A. (1997). The mentoring mindset: A constructivist perspective? *Mentoring & Tutoring, 5*(1), 14–24.

Murphy, C. (1992). Study groups foster schoolwide learning. *Educational Leadership, 50*(3), 71–74.

Noddings, N. (1984). *Caring.* Berkeley, CA: University of California Press.

Nolan, J., & Hoover, L. (2003). *Teacher supervision and evaluation: Theory into practice.* New York: John Wiley and Sons.

O'Brien, R. (1998). *An overview of the methodological approach of action research.* Available: http://www.web.net/~robrien/papers/arfinal.html.

Parsloe, E., & Wray, M. (2000). *Coaching and mentoring: Practical methods to improve learning.* London: Kogan Page.

Peterson, K. D. (2002, Summer). Positive or negative? *Journal of Staff Development, 23*(3), 1–6.

Pontz, B. (2003). *Beyond rhetoric: Adult learning policies and practices.* Paris: Organization for Economic and Cooperative Development.

Putnam, R., & Borko, H. (2000). Teacher learning: Implications from new perspectives on cognition. In B. Biddle, T. Good, & I. Goodson (Eds.), *Teachers and teaching, vol. 1.* Barcelona: Paidós.

Quick, T. L. (1992). *Successful team building.* New York: AMACOM.

Reason, P. (1994). Three approaches to participative inquiry. In N. Denzin & Y. Lincoln (Eds.), *Handbook of qualitative research.* Thousand Oaks, CA: Sage Publications.

Roderick, J. A. (1986). Dialogue writing: Context for reflecting on self as teacher and researcher. *Journal of Curriculum and Supervision, 1*(4), 305–315.

Sachs, J. (1999). *Teacher professional identity: Competing discourses, competing outcomes.* Sydney: University of Sydney. Available: http://www.aare.edu.au/99pap/sac99611.htm.

Sagor, R. (1992). *How to conduct collaborative action research.* Alexandria, VA: Association for Supervision and Curriculum Development

Schön, D. (1983). *The reflective practitioner: How professionals think in action.* New York: Basic Books.

Seidel, S. (1998). Wondering to be done: The collaborative assessment conference. In D. Allen (Ed.), *Assessing student learning: From grading to understanding.* New York: Teachers College Press.

Sergiovanni, T. J., & Starratt, R. J. (2002). *Supervision: A redefinition.* New York: McGraw Hill.

Showers, B. (1982). *Transfer of training: The contribution of coaching.* Eugene, OR: Center for Educational Policy and Management.

Shulman, L. S. (1987). Knowledge and teaching foundations of the new reforms. *Harvard Educational Review, 57*(1), 1–22.

Sparks, D. (2002). *Designing powerful staff development for teachers and principals.* Oxford, OH: National Staff Development Council.

Stigler, J., & Hiebert, J. (1999). *The teaching gap: Best ideas from the world's teachers for improving education in the classroom*. New York: The Free Press.

Sweeney, B. (1995). *Dialog journals: A mentor growth tool*. Available at: http://www.teachermentors.com/MCenter%20Site/dialogJ.html

Tomlinson, P. (1998). *Understanding mentoring: Reflective strategies for school-based teacher preparation*. Buckingham, England: Open University Press.

Tuckman, B. W. (1965). Developmental sequence in small groups. *Psychological Bulletin, 63*(6), 384–399.

Tuckman, B. W., & Jensen, M. A. C. (1977). Stages in small group development revisited. *Group and Organizational Studies, 2*, 419–427.

Tuhiwai Smith, L. (1999). *Decolonizing methodologies: Research and indigenous people*. London: Zed Books and University of Otago Press.

Tyack, D., & Tobin, W. (1994). The "grammar" of schooling: Why has it been so hard to change? *American Educational Research Journal, 31*(3), 453–479.

Umphrey, M. (2001). *Making field notes*. St. Ignatius, MT: The Montana Heritage Project. Available: http://www.edheritage.org/forms/fieldnotes.htm.

Vella, J. (1994). *Learning to listen, learning to teach: The power of dialogue in educating adults*. San Francisco: Jossey-Bass.

Weis, L., & Fine, M. (2000). *Speed bumps: A student-friendly guide to qualitative research*. New York: Teachers College Press.

Wenglinsky, H. (2000). *How teaching matters: Bringing the classroom back into discussions of teacher quality*. Princeton, NJ: Educational Testing Service.

Wertsch, J. (1999). *La mente en acción*. Buenos Aires: AIQUE.

West, W. (1996, Fall). Group learning in the workplace. *New Directions for Adult and Continuing Education, 71*, 51–60.

Wheelan, S. A. (1999). *Creating effective teams: A guide for members and leaders*. Thousand Oaks, CA: Sage Publications

Whitehead, J. (2001). *Reviewing educational research from the ground of educational practice: Constructing one's own living educational theories*. Available: http://www.actionresearch.net.

Wilcox, B. L., & Tomei, L. A. (1999). *Professional portfolios for teachers: A guide for learners, experts, and scholars*. Norwood, MA: Christopher Gordon Publishers.

Wlodkowski, R. J., & Ginsberg, M. (1995). *Diversity and motivation.* San Francisco: Jossey-Bass.

Woodward, T. (1993). *Models and metaphors in teacher training.* Cambridge: Cambridge University Press.

Zeichner, K., & Liston, D. (1996). *Reflective teaching: An introduction.* Mahwah, NJ: Lawrence Erlbaum and Associates.

Index

Page numbers followed by an *f* indicate reference to a figure.

Academy for Educational Development, 16–17
    action research, 60, 61, 62, 63, 65
    administrators, 152–155
    evaluation and, 155
    main duties of, 153
    management styles of, 153
    roles and functions of, 159*f*
    Teacher's Choice Framework and, 153
adult instruction, effective, 138–139
alternative grouping, 59
Association of Middle School Principals (AMSP), 143, 146
authoritative reflection, 92
awareness, 15–16, 18, 49, 63

Belbin, Meredith, 32

chairperson, 126–127
Chinese proverb, 128
classroom interactions, 89*f*
classroom observation, 80–96
    methods of, 87–92

classroom observation (*continued*)
    post-observation reflection protocol, 95–96
    preparation for, 85–87
    reflection, 92, 94–96
    stages of, 83–84
    teacher's movement, 90–92, 91*f*
clinical supervision, 83, 84
coached teacher, 83, 84, 85, 86
coaches, 78, 81, 83, 84, 85, 94
    See also peer coaching
coach's task, 87
collaborative action research
    effective questions for, 65
    objectives, 61
    process, 62–63
    steps of, 63–64
    Teacher's Choice Framework and, 73–74
collaborative learning activities for extended courses, 150–151*f*
collaborative teams, 26–33
collaborative work, 24–25
commitment, as phase of career, 8, 50
communication, 72, 73
community needs, 63
competency-based model, 55
concentration, 49

177

About the Author

Gabriel Díaz-Maggioli is a teacher educator at the National Teacher's Training College and at International House in Montevideo, Uruguay, as well as a national supervisor in the Uruguayan Department of Education's Secondary Schools Unit. He has acted as consultant for the Uruguayan Department of Education's National Educational Reform Project in the areas of curriculum design and teacher development. During the 2002–2003 academic year he was a Fulbright Hubert H. Humphrey Fellow at Penn State's Departments of Curriculum and Supervision and Curriculum and Instruction. He can be reached by e-mail at gabrieldiazmaggioli@hotmail.com.

Related ASCD Resources

At the time of publication, the following ASCD resources were available. ASCD stock numbers are noted in parentheses.

Books

Capturing the Wisdom of Practice by Giselle O. Martin-Kniep (#199254)

Educators as Learners: Creating a Professional Learning Community in Your School (2000) by Penelope J. Wald and Michael S. Castleberry (#100005)

A New Vision for Staff Development (1997) by Dennis Sparks and Stephanie Hirsh (#197018)

Student Achievement Through Staff Development, 3rd ed. (2002) by Bruce R. Joyce and Beverly Showers (#102003)

Multimedia

Analytic Processes for School Leaders: An ASCD Action Tool by Cynthia T. Richetti and Benjamin B. Tregoe (#701016)

Videos

Action Research: Inquiry, Reflection, and Decision Making by Carl Glickman and Emily Calhoun (4 videos) (#495037)

Improving Instruction Through Observation and Feedback (3 videos and a facilitator's guide) (#402058)

Teacher Portfolios by Mary Dietz (2 videos and a facilitator's guide) (#497026)

For more information, visit us on the World Wide Web (http://www.ascd.org), send an e-mail message to member@ascd.org, call the ASCD Service Center (1-800-933-ASCD or 703-575-5400, then press 2), send a fax to 703-575-5400, or write to Information Services, ASCD, 1703 N. Beauregard St., Alexandria, VA 22311-1714 USA.